ADDICT
IN THE FAMILY

ADDICT
IN THE FAMILY

Stories of Loss, Hope,
and Recovery

BEVERLY CONYERS

HAZELDEN

Hazelden
Center City, Minnesota 55012-0176

1-800-328-0094
1-651-213-4590 (Fax)
www.hazelden.org

Library of Congress Cataloging-in-Publication Data

Conyers, Beverly.
    Addict in the family : stories of loss, hope, and recovery / Beverly Conyers.
      p.   cm.
    Includes bibliographical references.
    ISBN 13: 978-1-56838-999-8
     1. Alcoholics—Family relationships.   2. Narcotic addicts—Family
relationships.   3. Alcoholics—Rehabilitation.   4. Narcotic addicts—
Rehabilitation.   I. Title.
HV5132.C645 2003
362.292'3—dc21

                                             2003050829

10 09 08   6 5 4

Cover design by David Spohn
Interior design by Stanton Publication Services, Inc.
Typesetting by Stanton Publication Services, Inc.

Author's note
All the stories in this book are based on actual experiences and personal interviews.
Names and certain facts have been changed to protect the anonymity of the men and
women who shared their stories for this book.

This book is dedicated to the Tuesday night group with heartfelt appreciation —and to my daughter with love.

CONTENTS

ACKNOWLEDGMENTS

Dozens of people have very generously shared their intimate stories about addiction and recovery with me. Without their honesty and courage, I could not have written this book. In addition, many professionals in the treatment community contributed their knowledge and insight, including Debbie Galinski, L.R.C.; Barbara K. George, L.M.H.C.; Dayna Gladstein, L.I.C.S.W., C.D.P.; Joseph Hyde, L.M.H.C., C.A.S.; and Bert Pepper, M.D. To all, thank you.

INTRODUCTION

It is a Thursday night in late November. The sky is blanketed with low, thick clouds, the air heavy with impending rain. Bare branches of old trees carve faint silhouettes in a world of black and gray, relieved only by a single light above a narrow door and a horizontal row of five small square windows close to the ground and lit from within.

Inside the church basement, thirteen people sit around two rectangular folding tables pushed together. On the tables are books and pamphlets, a few bottles of water, and a box of tissues. The room is brightly lit by suspended fluorescent tubes, revealing pale yellow concrete walls, a green-and-white tile floor, and thin white curtains on the windows. The lights emit a faint whine, punctuated by the chirps and occasional clangs of three old radiators. No one pays any attention to the noises. All eyes are on Dot, a woman in her sixties with soft, peach-tinted hair, a tired face made up in muted shades of pink, and sad blue eyes. She is, in her way, an attractive woman, with a large, soft body and a kindly face—the kind of face you associate with grandmothers who have spent their lives looking after their families and putting others first.

Tonight, Dot clutches a tissue in her hands. She announces to her support group, "He almost drowned in beef stew." Her voice holds amazement, as well as grief. "Honest to God. I was in the front room watching television with my husband. And something in the back of my mind says, 'David's been awful quiet,' so I went out to the kitchen, and there he was with his face in a bowl of stew. He didn't seem to be breathing. So I lifted up his head, and there was gravy and little bits of meat all over his face. 'You gotta stop this,' I said to him." She twists the tissue in her hands. "Honest to God. If I hadn't checked up on him, he would have drowned."

She is speaking of her thirty-six-year-old son, the baby of the family, the one who, as a little boy, had been the clown who made everyone laugh. A person couldn't be around David for five minutes without smiling at some silly thing he said or did—like the time during the third-grade Christmas pageant when he stood on stage with a dozen or so other children and sang both verses of "Silent Night" with his eyes crossed. She had wanted to kill him but ended up giggling instead.

Even now he can make her laugh, though tears are never far behind. David has been a heroin addict for eleven years and on methadone for the past three. She knows he still shoots up on occasion, but his latest thing is pills. He's been prescribed painkillers for a knee injury he got from falling down a flight of stairs. The pills are morphine based. David has gone through a month's prescription in four days.

"I locked them up in my safe, but somehow he got into them," she tells her group. "A drug addict can get anything if he makes up his mind to do it, you know."

A few heads nod in understanding.

"The thing is, I didn't say anything to my husband. I didn't want to get him going, because he would've been off the wall. I just told David to go wash his face and put on a clean shirt." She shakes her head. "I'm learning."

There's an extended silence. No one rushes to fill it. It's as if the group has all the time in the world to think things over and wait for Dot to conclude her tale. One woman surreptitiously wipes her eyes, while a man gazes grimly at a distant wall. The sound of breathing blends with the faint whine of the lights. After two or three minutes, Dot says, "I thought it would be different when he came home this time. You know?"

She laughs, but there is no humor in the sound.

A few minutes later a man is talking. He is a big man, broad shouldered and physically powerful. He wears metal-framed glasses with thick lenses that magnify his eyes, giving him an oddly vulnerable look. He owns his own business and is thinking about retiring in a few years. What is utmost in his mind tonight is his daughter Lila. She is twenty-two and has already caused him more heartache than his other three kids combined. After almost dying of anorexia in high school, she discovered pot in college and quickly moved on to crack cocaine and heroin. She dropped out of school in her sophomore year and moved with her boyfriend a couple of states away.

"She was home last week for Thanksgiving," he says, pushing his glasses up the bridge of his nose. "She looked pretty good. Thin but not skinny, thank God. I wouldn't want to go through that again." He squints, searching for words. "My wife said she was high, but I couldn't tell. She wasn't falling into her plate anyway."

There are a few chuckles.

"I hated to see her go back, but I know she has to live her own life. I can't live it for her." Some heads nod in agreement.

"Anyway, my wife was changing the sheets after Lila left, and she found some clean needles under the mattress. I wanted to throw them in the garbage, but my wife said no. She said the next time Lila comes home we want her to have clean needles, don't we?"

A few people squirm, as if their chairs have become uncomfortable. "I'm still thinking about that one," he says. "I mean, I guess so. But I don't know."

The hands on the big round wall clock move on. "I could kill my sister for what she's doing to my parents!" exclaims a pretty, young woman. "I told him I'm not bailing him out this time," asserts a middle-aged man. "I went through it with my daughter, and now it's starting all over again with my grandson," says a woman with white hair. Her voice is angry, but before she finishes speaking, her anger dissolves into tears.

One by one the members of the group speak. They talk of children, husbands and wives, parents, brothers and sisters. They share tales of deception, theft, jail, homelessness, institutions, sickness, and poverty—bleak narratives that document the destructive course of substance abuse. At the heart of every story lies the pain of having an addict in the family.

Few experiences in life quite match the feelings of horror, fear, helplessness, and grief that families experience when someone they love becomes addicted to alcohol or other drugs. They watch in dismay as the addict becomes alienated from the family and undergoes profound changes. Activities that once brought the addict pleasure are abandoned, old friends are pushed away, and the addict withdraws into a world that is inaccessible to anyone who tries to help.

Families ask themselves if their loved one is gone forever, replaced by an untrustworthy, soulless being like the empty-eyed creatures in *Invasion of the Body Snatchers*. More urgently, they ask themselves what they can do to effect a "cure" and get their loved one back to normal. They hope for a quick fix. Maybe detox and a good treatment facility will be all it takes. All too often, they end up joining the addict on the merry-go-round of denial, anger, confusion, and blame.

It's a depressing business, one that's experienced annually by millions of American families. In 1999, the National Household Survey on Drug Abuse revealed that an estimated 10.3 million Americans were dependent on either alcohol or illicit drugs. Chances are someone in your family is among them. If that is the case, you have my sympathy. I have been in your shoes. The heroin addiction of my own daughter has motivated me to write this book. After the initial shock of learning about her addiction, I began to look for answers to overwhelming questions: Had I caused her addiction? How could I have been so blind as not to see it earlier? What was it doing to her health, her happiness, her future? Was there any hope for her recovery? How could I help her get well? Was it possible to find any peace of mind and have a life of my own?

I found that while there were many books that dealt with various aspects of addiction and recovery, none seemed to fill my need for reliable information and helpful advice from people who have endured a similar crisis. I decided to expand my research to substance-abuse counselors, to other families of addicts, and to addicts themselves—both active users and those in recovery. This book is the compilation of what I have learned.

It does not promise simple solutions or definitive answers to all your questions. That would be an impossible promise to keep. What it does offer is education and support in the form of practical information, advice from others who have been there, and the healing power of shared experiences. The real-life stories that people have shared in this book are intended to do much more than illustrate a point. They are intended to reduce the feelings of isolation often experienced by families who are coping with addiction and to be a source of comfort, insight, understanding, and hope.

ONE

A FAMILY DISEASE

When Shelly began to talk about her daughter, she seemed to visibly shrink. Her shoulders slumped, her head drooped, and even the muscles of her pretty face went slack. She suddenly looked ten years older than the chic, petite blond who had walked through the door only moments before.

"I know this is hard for you," I apologized.

She waved her hand and paused to gather her thoughts.

We were seated at a corner table set apart from the others in the bookstore café. Around us people chatted, laughed, or read one of the books or magazines set out for customers' enjoyment. There was a pleasant smell of coffee and baked goods.

The café was one of my favorite places, full of warmth and life. But in our little corner, the air was weighted with sadness. "If someone had told me two years ago that I'd be having this conversation, I'd have said they were out of their mind," she said with an attempted laugh. "Colleen was always the most responsible, considerate, and *respectable* girl you could ever meet. I don't think she ever even got a parking ticket."

I shook my head in sympathy.

"She had a perfect life. Everything she ever wanted. Her husband adored her. They had that sweet house and those beautiful babies." Her voice caught a little, and she swallowed some water before almost hissing out her next words: "And then she met that bum!"

"That bum" was a twenty-nine-year-old drug dealer named Marlon. How he and Colleen had met isn't clear, but soon after, her life took a 180-degree turn for the worse. She experimented with cocaine and in seemingly no time at all was hooked on crack. At first her husband had no explanation for Colleen's wild mood swings, evasiveness, irritability, and occasional incoherence. He urged her to see a doctor, but on the day of her appointment, he came home to find a note taped to the fridge: *Jeff, I'm sick of living for everyone else. I'm going to start living for myself.*

"She dropped the kids off at my house that day," Shelly remembered. "I thought she looked tired. And thin. Awfully thin. But I had no idea anything was going on. Jeff didn't say anything until later."

Colleen moved in with her dealer and quit her job as an insurance claims adjuster, a position she had held for more than four years. At first she visited Jeff and the children three or four times a week, but the visits tapered off to no more than once or twice a month.

Shelly speculated, "I think Jeff was relieved, in a way, because her behavior was so unpredictable that she upset the children. I think she scared them." Shelly's eyes filled with tears. "Can you imagine? My grandchildren being scared of their own mother."

After nearly a year of begging Colleen to get help, Jeff filed for divorce and was awarded full custody of their children. Although the divorce was not final when Shelly and I talked, she was certain that reconciliation would be impossible. "I think he hates her for what she's done to the kids," she said. "And all the rest of it. The lies, the stealing. He won't let her in the house anymore. Not since she walked out with the CD player and the VCR. We *know* where they ended up. At some pawnshop and up her nose."

Shelly's voice was harsh, but behind the anger was, I suspected, boundless grief. Her next words confirmed my thoughts. "Where will it end?" she whispered. "I think about it every waking moment of my life. No matter where I am or what I do, she's right there with me, filling up my head. Last month, my husband and I left for a weekend to get away from everything. We shouldn't have bothered. I was like a zombie. I was sick with fear the whole time. I can't stop worrying about what's going to happen to my daughter. I know she's done horrible, despicable things. But it's the drugs making her do it. It really is. Underneath it all she's still a good person."

She wiped her eyes with a napkin. "I'm so afraid. She's my baby, and I'm so scared she's not going to make it."

Her worry is not unwarranted. The National Center for Health Statistics (NCHS) reported 19,102 street-drug-related deaths in 1999, up from 14,843 in 1996, excluding accidents, homicides, AIDS, and other potential consequences of drug addiction. The Drug Abuse Warning Network (DAWN), which tracks drug abuse in forty-one major metropolitan areas across the nation, reported 601,776 drug-related emergency room visits in 2000, up from 527,000 in 1997. From 1999 to 2000, the total drug-related emergency room visits increased 20 percent in patients between twelve and seventeen and 13 percent in those between eighteen and twenty-five. The numbers of alcohol-related deaths, accidents, and diseases are even higher. NCHS reported 19,358 alcohol-induced deaths in 1999 and 26,552 deaths from chronic liver disease and cirrhosis. Liver disease, often the result of chronic alcoholism, is the twelfth leading cause of death in the United States.

Addiction to alcohol or other drugs plunges its victims into lives of poverty, homelessness, crime, and jail. It stunts emotional and spiritual growth and ravages mental and physical health. Indeed, the consequences of the disease of addiction—and most mental health professionals agree that it *is* a disease—are as potentially devastating as those of most other major illnesses.

But the impact of addiction does not end there. For almost every addict who is mired in this terrible disease, others—a mother or father, a child or spouse, an aunt or uncle or grandparent, a brother or sister—are suffering too. Families are the hidden victims of addiction, enduring enormous levels of stress and pain. They suffer sleepless nights, deep anxiety, and physical exhaustion brought on by worry and desperation. They lie awake for hours on end as fear for their loved one's safety crowds out any possibility of sleep. They live each day with a weight inside that drags them down. Unable to laugh or smile, they are sometimes filled with bottled-up anger or a constant sadness that keeps them on the verge of tears.

Despite their suffering, families of addicts seldom receive the kind of support commonly extended to families of, say, cancer patients or stroke victims. Instead, they conceal their pain in the face of the all-too-common beliefs that addicts have only themselves to blame for their troubles, that addicts could cure themselves if they really wanted to, and that addicts' families probably did something "wrong" to cause the problem in the first place. Many families of addicts share these views, which only adds to their unhappiness.

"I could never tell anyone at work what's going on with

Colleen," Shelly admitted. "They'd all look down on me. It's too horrible, too shameful."

Todd, a successful small-business owner, described his own feelings of guilt and shame about his twenty-eight-year-old son's alcoholism. "Watching my son throw his life away has been the most difficult experience of my life," he said. "The worst part is that I feel at fault. If I'd done things differently, he might not be where he is today, which is basically nowhere."

Searching for the root cause of the problem, Todd explained how he had worked long hours while his son was growing up. "I was gone three, four days every week. Maybe he thought I didn't love him. I don't know. Maybe he needed more discipline. Whatever it was, Mike went wild at an early age. By the time he was fourteen, he was emptying out the liquor cabinet and filling the bottles with water. I wanted to take a strap to him. That's what my father would've done. But his mother wouldn't hear of it and thought he needed counseling. Counseling! Forty thousand dollars of counseling! Mike's all grown up now except he's still like a little kid. I can't tell you the number of cars he has smashed up. And the jobs. Can't hold a job for more than a week. Of course he still lives with us. I don't see how he'll ever make it on his own."

Todd scratched his head, causing the silver-brown hair to stand on end. He took a long time getting to his next point, which for him seemed to be the most difficult. "I listen to our friends talk about what their kids are doing: graduating from college, starting careers, getting married and settling down. Normal stuff, you know? I just change the subject. What did they know that I didn't? Where did I go wrong?"

Todd was voicing important questions that haunt anyone who has ever loved an addict: "What did I do that caused this

problem?" and "What can I do to fix it?" He had not yet discovered the simple truth about addiction that is so hard for
families to accept: You didn't cause it, you can't control it,
and you can't cure it.

It is normal to want to help those we love, especially
when they are faced with a crippling condition such as addiction. However, the burden of guilt, the sense that we have
somehow "caused" the addiction, can intensify our resolve to
"cure" the addict, spurring us on to sometimes unhealthy and
even counterproductive levels of involvement in the addict's
life. Parents, especially, look back on all the regrettable but
inevitable mistakes of parenthood and feel a heavy sense of
responsibility.

Even if families recognize that they did not cause the addiction, most feel a desire, even an obligation, to do everything possible to help their loved one. As families assume
more of the burden of addiction, they may spend enormous
amounts of time and money in their attempts to get their
loved one off alcohol or other drugs. Often, the harder they
try, the more the addict resists their efforts.

This tug-of-war can last for years, with continued addiction and emotional exhaustion as the unfortunate results.

THE ELUSIVE CURE

Missy, a divorced mother of two teenage girls, was engaged
to a landscaper's assistant who played guitar in a local band
most Friday and Saturday nights. She had met him at a club
and was immediately attracted to his blond good looks. Early
in the relationship, he had admitted to an on-and-off drug
problem. After living with him for three months, she realized
the problem was mostly on and that the drug was heroin.

"I felt physically sick when I found out," she told me. "I

mean, you hear all these stories about junkies, about how they'd kill their own mother for a fix, and here I'd brought this man into my house and made him a part of my family. At first I wanted to break it off, to end it right there. But I realized he was the same person I'd fallen in love with, except he had this big problem. I thought that maybe I could help him, that with my love and support he could get better."

Missy tried to take charge of her fiancé's behavior. She got him to check into a rehab hospital for thirty days, and when he came home, she began to monitor his actions. She was afraid to let him out of her sight. When he did go out, she wanted to know where he was going, whom he was with, and when he'd be home. While he was gone, she went through his personal belongings, checking for hidden drugs. After only a week, she found a syringe. When she confronted him, he became angry. He said the syringe had been there a long time and that she had no right to go through his things. Worse, he said her hounding was making him crave drugs.

Missy tried to back off, but her suspicions ate away at her. Before long, she found herself following him around. Once, when he was parked in front of an apartment house where she suspected he bought drugs, she blocked his car with her own and waited for him to come out. He was furious when he saw her outside. They had a loud and prolonged argument in the street. "I must have looked like a crazy person," she said, blushing at the memory. "In a way I was. I was out of my mind. I thought that if I screamed, nagged, or threatened him enough he'd get clean. It didn't work."

In a way Missy was fortunate. She soon grew tired of her fiancé's increasingly irresponsible behavior and broke off the relationship. It is usually much harder for parents and other close family members to shut the addict out of their lives. Instead, when confronted with addiction, families are often drawn into painful, lengthy, and costly attempts to help the addict get better.

"We could have bought New York with the money we spent on our daughter," declared Elaine, a schoolteacher whose husband owned a thriving real estate business. I met with her in her home, where a collage of photographs of her daughter at various ages hung on a wall in the living room. She was a pretty girl with a wide smile.

"She started with pot and alcohol when she was just a kid," Elaine explained. "When we found out, we had her committed to a rehab program out of state. She was there for six months, and when she came home, we thought we had the problem licked. She seemed so much better. Then she moved on to cocaine, so we sent her to a different place—someplace even more expensive. We figured the first program wasn't right for her. We just needed to find the right fit."

Elaine didn't realize it, but she and her husband had taken supporting roles in a painful drama that would drag on for the next eight years. Unlike a real dramatic play, however, each new act was a repetition of the first: their daughter would check into rehab, she'd be clean for a while, and then she would relapse and end up in rehab again.

"It was so discouraging," Elaine sighed. "And so predictable. She'd be clean for a while, sometimes more than a year. But she'd always ended up going back to the stuff. We were out of our minds with worry."

In addition to rehab, Elaine and her husband tried everything they could think of to get their daughter off drugs, including rewards and bribery. "We'd say things like, 'Stay clean and we'll give you a car, or we'll pay your rent, or we'll send you on a nice relaxing vacation to someplace nice like the Bahamas.' I tried rewarding her for every week she was clean by paying for a day spa, a new haircut, or buying her clothes or jewelry." Elaine laughed ruefully. "It didn't work. Eventually I'd notice she wasn't wearing a necklace she especially liked or that I hadn't seen a certain ring in a while. Things were falling apart again. She was hitting the pawnshops."

Other families engage in equally earnest but futile attempts to solve their loved one's addiction problems. They make counseling appointments for the addict, try to find the addict a job, take charge of the addict's grooming and cleanliness, drive the addict to Alcoholics Anonymous (AA) or Narcotics Anonymous (NA) meetings, throw out the addict's alcohol or other drugs when they find them, supervise the addict's diet, and try to prevent the addict from hanging out with the "wrong" people. They watch the addict's every mood with an eagle eye and gauge the addict's condition by observing sleep patterns, appetite, pupil size, skin tone, and day-to-day behavior. They nag, scold, threaten, and beg the addict to get clean and sober.

For all their tears and heartache and desperately good intentions, most families of addicts are defeated in the end. Addicts persist in their self-destructive, addictive behavior until something *within themselves*—something quite apart from anyone else's efforts—changes so radically that the desire for the high is dulled and ultimately deadened by the desire for a better life.

The truth most families eventually discover is that no one can cure another person's addiction. Only addicts can do that for themselves.

Does this mean that families have no role to play in the miraculous process of recovery? On the contrary. Families can have a powerful impact on their addict's struggle for recovery. Studies have shown time and again that addicts who feel connected to a family that supports their recovery (even

if that family is just one person) have a better chance of staying clean than those who believe that no one cares.

However, there is a catch. The families themselves must
be healthy if they hope to have a positive influence on their
loved one. Although this may seem self-evident, it is easy for
families to lose sight of this truth as the disease of addiction
threatens their own mental health. Family members can lose
their ability to think clearly and behave rationally when they
are confronted with the addict's world.

The process of addiction creates an alternative reality in
the addict's mind. Thinking becomes distorted and values get
twisted as the search for the next high takes precedence over
every other consideration. Families, in their interactions
with the addict, get caught up in the insanity of the disease.
Lines between reality and fantasy blur as families, in their
desperate attempts to control and cure the addiction, begin
to think and behave in ways that, upon reflection, make no
sense. The more enmeshed family members become in their
addict's life, the more twisted their thinking is likely to become. As a result, their efforts to help the addict grow increasingly futile, and their own well-being is compromised.
A relationship that many professionals call codependence is
established, harming both the addict and his or her family.

To prevent this unhealthy relationship from occurring, or
to extricate themselves from such a relationship, families
must arm themselves with as much knowledge about addiction as possible. They must understand what they *can* do to
support the recovery process and learn successful strategies
for coping with addictive behaviors. They must recognize
common mistakes that may actually prolong addiction and
avoid getting trapped in unhealthy patterns. Perhaps most
important, they must reaffirm the value of their own lives

and focus on their own peace of mind—regardless of what their addicted loved one does.

One of the most startling statements I heard in the early days of dealing with my daughter's addiction came from a recovering addict who told me, "Even if your daughter is living on the streets, you can still have happy days." It seemed unbelievable to me, yet after many months, I came to see the wisdom of that remark.

None of this is easy. Addicts' families walk an unhappy path that is strewn with many pitfalls and false starts. Mistakes are inevitable. Pain is inevitable. But so are growth and wisdom and serenity if families approach addiction with an open mind, a willingness to learn, and the acceptance that recovery, like addiction itself, is a long and complex process. Families should never give up hope for recovery—for recovery can and does happen every day. Nor should they stop living their own lives while they wait for that miracle of recovery to occur. As a first step toward understanding the processes of addiction and recovery, the next chapter looks at some common addictive behaviors.

T W O

THE STRANGER YOU LOVE

All addicts' stories are heartbreaking in their own unique ways. But if you hear enough of these stories, you begin to realize that they are also distressingly similar. They follow a predictable pattern of experimentation, addiction, and eventual loss of everything most of us hold dear, including family, home, job, and personal values. Addicts become estranged from the nonaddicted world and seem not to mind when they are reduced to circumstances that would be intolerable to almost anyone who is thinking clearly. My own daughter was a prime example.

A heroin addict at age twenty-three, my daughter and her boyfriend, a fellow addict, were evicted from their apartment for not paying their rent. In the four months they had lived there, their apartment had become almost uninhabitable. The filthy bathroom contained a phone book that they used for toilet paper. The living room was a chaotic jumble of dirty dishes and soiled clothing and bedding. The bedroom floor was covered with animal feces from their cats and ferret.

They eventually moved in with friends for a short time and then to the back of their car, a small station wagon. By that time they had lost or sold most of their possessions.

Only a few items of clothing and some bedding remained. My daughter always wore the same long-sleeved shirt stained with sweat; the cuffs and sleeves were speckled with dots and streaks of blood. Her shoes smelled like rotten meat.

Yet when I confronted her about her situation, she insisted that nothing was wrong. "A lot of people live in their cars, Mom," she said, as if it were the most normal thing in the world. "We're going to get a new apartment next week. This is not a big deal." She denied the addiction outright.

As sickened as I was by her situation, I did not fully realize that I was dealing with someone who inhabited a different mental world than my own. Only later did I begin to see that we shared no common ground, that it was impossible for us to communicate because she had lost touch with everyday reality, and that my daughter had, in fact, become a stranger.

Most families of addicts experience similar feelings about their loved one. They say such things as "I don't even know who he is anymore" and "I look into her eyes and it's like there's no one there." One mother of an addict said to me with tears in her eyes, "What a terrible disease this is. It takes away our kids."

People sometimes claim that addicts have "lost their souls." What they mean is that the addicts no longer seem to care about anything but their drug of choice, that they have become untrustworthy, and that their value system seems bizarre or nonexistent.

Families experience a tremendous sense of loss as they see their loved one, who once possessed certain defining characteristics such as a good sense of humor or a strong work ethic or an affectionate nature, lose these positive traits. Indeed, individuality deteriorates as the addict takes on behaviors that are typical of other addicts, behaviors that are aimed at achieving one end: the next high.

Recognizable addictive behaviors, present to a greater or lesser degree in most addicts, emerge as addiction takes hold. They are the result of a subconscious process in which new thought patterns are adopted to facilitate addiction. Addicts do not consciously decide to change their behavior. Rather, the process of change occurs at a deeper level, a result of the marvelous human capacity to adapt to altered circumstances. The addicts, not realizing what is happening, begin to think and behave in ways that may have been foreign before the addiction took hold, but that now seem natural and even necessary. Their brains have been biologically and chemically altered.

Families generally sense the changes in their loved one but do not fully appreciate the depth of those changes. They may continue to treat the addict as they have in the past, only to find their interactions with the addict increasingly confusing. They cannot find any solid ground in the changed relationship as the addict begins to exhibit a disturbing repertoire of addictive behaviors.

Foremost among these addictive behaviors is denial.

DENIAL

It is not uncommon in our society to hear someone described as being "in denial." This condition is generally understood to mean that the person in question is unwilling or unable to face the truth about a particular circumstance. Who among us hasn't been in denial about something, whether it's our relationships, our diet, our spending habits, or some other troubling aspect of our lives? Many families of addicts, including myself, deny their loved one's addiction for a long time before circumstances force them to face it. Denial seems to be a natural human response to situations we are unready or unable to cope with.

When applied to addiction, however, denial is taken to the extreme. Denial permeates all of addicts' thinking, blotting out reality and replacing it with a twisted perception that *everything* is other than what it is. The denial is most obvious when addicts are challenged to evaluate their own situation. They immediately deny that they have a problem and insist that they can control or stop their use of alcohol or other drugs whenever they choose.

Denise, a secretary whose seventeen-year-old son was hooked on heroin, described talking to him about the problem: "At first he said I was crazy, that I was imagining things. He kept telling me to leave him alone. He was really angry. But a friend of his had told me he was addicted, so I kept after him. He finally admitted to snorting heroin 'a little bit' at parties and things like that. He acted like it was nothing. Then he started stealing money from my pocketbook. All that time I was confused because I felt things were bad, but he kept assuring me he had things under control. Then he sold his guitar, and I knew I couldn't go along with his denial anymore. I forced him to see a counselor. I found out he was shooting up four times a day. Even then, he still insisted he could stop anytime he wanted."

Peggy, married to a police officer hooked on cocaine, faced a similar experience. "He was spending every cent he made on cocaine," she said. "He stopped paying the bills, stopped buying groceries, so I had to take on all the household expenses. I kept threatening to walk out on him, and he kept saying I was crazy. He didn't have a problem. He was just fine. You know something? I honestly think he believed it. I don't think he had a clue about what was happening to him."

The pattern of denial that Peggy and Denise confronted is typical of most addicts. Denial is the mental mechanism that enables addicts to give up more and more of the things that are truly valuable in life in favor of an artificial and fleeting sense of well-being induced by a chemical. In other words, denial is the foundation of addiction, the fertile soil in which it grows and flourishes. Denial provides the comforting delusion that everything is all right, smoothing the way for addicts as they wind deeper into their downward spiral.

A truism about addicts is that they will always deny their addiction or, if forced to admit it, they will minimize its depth. They consistently say such things as "I can stop any time I want" and "I only use it occasionally" and "I don't need help—there's nothing wrong." Even when everyone around them knows that addiction is destroying their lives, addicts will deny that they have a problem.

The depth of their denial does not stop there. As addiction takes it inevitable toll, addicts will also deny the severity of the consequences. Even as their world crumbles around them, as everything of value is stripped away, they will claim that their losses are not of much consequence. Their entire belief system is altered by the power of denial.

Jerry and Teresa, who had recently celebrated their thirtieth wedding anniversary, described their horror as their only daughter endured one tragedy after another without apparent concern. Their daughter was a nurse, a single mother in a committed relationship with her child's father. She became addicted to prescription drugs and lost her job. Soon afterward, she was arrested for forging prescriptions, then for shoplifting, and finally for prostitution. Over the course of several years, she spent many months in jail and lost her car, her apartment, and most of her possessions. Her boyfriend left her, and ultimately she lost custody of her child.

"It wasn't until we were awarded custody of our grandchild that I finally realized just how sick her thinking had become," Teresa said. "As she was being led off to prison and we were raising her child, her only comment was 'Well, it's only for nine months. I don't see what you're making such a big deal about.' Nine months! Nine minutes would have been too long for me to endure a situation like that. But she didn't seem to get it."

The power and importance of denial cannot be overstated when it comes to understanding addiction. Even when addicts are facing life on the streets or incarceration, they will deny that addiction is the root cause of their troubles. Their perception becomes so distorted by denial that they may be truly unable to comprehend the disaster that has befallen them.

DISHONESTY

Closely related to denial is dishonesty. Dishonesty encompasses the evasiveness and lies, big and small, that addicts employ in their attempts to control their world, as well as the criminal behavior they may engage in to sustain their habit. A small joke that hints at the denial and dishonesty at the heart of the addict's world goes like this: An alcoholic will steal your wallet and lie about it. A drug addict will steal your wallet, then help you look for it.

Families dealing with addicted loved ones are dealing with liars. This statement may sound harsh, but it is almost always true. Addicts become master liars very early on in their substance abuse. They learn to lie to conceal their habit. They lie so they can feed their habit. They lie to maintain their self-delusion about their habit. And finally, they lie because lying itself has become a habit.

One of the most difficult and painful aspects of my relationship with my daughter was trying to discern when she was lying and when she was telling the truth. Many of her lies seemed senseless to me, intended merely to keep me off balance or at a distance. Often in those early, edgy months of her attempted recovery, there were moments in which I believed genuine honesty had been achieved, only to later discover that whatever she had been telling me was pure fabrication. There came a time when I simply stopped believing anything she said.

Many families have had similar experiences. "I was worried about Abby for years before I learned about her crack addiction," said her father, a cross-country truck driver. "I knew something wasn't right, and I kept telling myself it was depression or PMS or growing pains—anything but drugs. I remember asking one of her friends if my daughter had a drug problem. Word got back to Abby, and she was furious, like I was the worst dad in the world. How could I even think such a thing about her? I felt like a jerk. Another time, I noticed a radio, TV, and other things of hers were missing. She said a friend had borrowed them. I remember saying half-jokingly that I hoped she wasn't pawning them. She asked what did I think she was? What kind of person goes around pawning things? Of course, I later found out that was exactly what she was doing. Everything she'd told me was a lie. But she was so convincing."

One mother described coming home to find a note from her son, who had been in recovery for some time. It said that he was out to lunch with his sponsor, the sponsor's treat. The mother felt good until the sponsor called that same day, asking for her son. The sponsor knew nothing about a lunch date and had not seen her son in some time.

Another mother remembered her daughter's elaborate lie about someone she had met in a support group: "She told me she'd met a nice girl, a Hispanic woman named Maria who had three children. She told me this whole story about

Maria's life and the hard times she'd been through and how she lived with her mother and on and on. I eventually found out there was no Maria. My daughter had made the whole thing up."

Another woman summed up her exasperation with her husband's lies by saying, "If he told me the sun was shining and I could see it with my own eyes, I still wouldn't believe him."

Lying not only conceals or minimizes an addiction problem, but it also allows addicts to pretend that life is the way they wish it could be. Perhaps creating a make-believe world helps them feel better in some small, untouched core of their being. They may also lie to gain approval or to tell their families what they think their families want to hear. Although so much about the addicts' personalities is altered by addiction, the human need for approval is strong and may well be a motivator behind some of the lies. However, regardless of their motives, when addicts lie, they undermine the core of trust that forms the basis of any healthy relationship. They create a huge gulf between themselves and their families, who end up feeling hurt, confused, and vulnerable.

Another facet of dishonesty is criminal activity. While not all addicts will turn to crime, most of them will cross the line into illegal activities at some point during the course of their addiction (that is, in addition to obtaining and using controlled substances).

My daughter and her boyfriend, for example, knowingly wrote a number of bad checks before local merchants caught on to them.

A former neighbor's husband, who unbeknownst to her had progressed from being a weekend cocaine user to a full-time heroin addict, repeatedly pawned the family's televisions and stereo equipment and claimed they were stolen. "I always wondered why ours was the only house that kept getting broken into," she recalled.

A mother of a crack addict kept her jewelry in a safe in the trunk of her car. "It was the only way I could think of to keep my daughter from stealing it," she said.

A father learned that his cocaine-addicted son had cleaned out the family checking account. "He's not living with us anymore, but I still hide the credit cards and keep my checkbooks and financial papers at work now in case he stops by the house," he told me.

Stories of theft, from the ten-dollar bill that disappears from someone's wallet to jewelry and other valuables that wind up in pawnshops, are common in families of addicts. Shoplifting something to pawn is also common among addicts. This activity often brings them to the attention of the local police. "My daughter was never arrested for drugs," one mother said, "but she went to jail three times for shoplifting." One addict described a profitable variation on common shoplifting: an item is stolen from a store and then returned for a cash refund. "Not all stores will do it," she said, "but if you find a store that does, it pays better than pawnshops."

Prostitution is the last resort for some addicts and is especially painful for most parents to acknowledge. A father of a crack addict expressed the feelings of many parents when he said, "I felt dead inside when I found out. I was numb for weeks. I couldn't accept the thought of my little girl out there turning tricks."

Because of the blurring effects of dishonesty and denial, addicts themselves are able to rationalize and minimize the corrupting influence of substance abuse. Often they seem unaware that their values have deteriorated. Families observe the downward slide with a growing sense of helplessness, a condition that works to the addicts' advantage.

MANIPULATION

Manipulation is an attempt to get others to fulfill our desires. It's a skill that many humans learn early on. For example, babies learn how to use tears or smiles to get their needs met, and toddlers and young children throw tantrums, pout, whine, beg, and wheedle to get their way. Adults, too, often try to manipulate others, sometimes without even realizing they are doing it. While some forms of manipulation may be relatively harmless, highly manipulative adults are almost universally viewed with distaste.

Addicts are master manipulators. No matter how irrational and self-defeating their behavior may seem, addicts often get just what they want from those who care most deeply about them. Like other manipulative people, the tools they most often use are fear, guilt, and pity.

Families suffer a great deal of fear when a loved one succumbs to addiction. They fear public humiliation, the disgrace of having an addict in the family. They fear for the addict's future, for the loss of home, health, and income. If the addict is a parent, they fear for the well-being of the addict's children. And almost universally, they fear for the addict's life.

One father put it succinctly: "We're afraid our daughter is going to die."

Another parent said, "We were convinced they were going to find her body in a Dumpster someday."

A mother said of her son, "My biggest fear is that he'll end up living on the streets, that he'll become one of those bums you see lying in a doorway somewhere, that people will just step over him like he's a piece of trash."

A sister of an alcoholic told me, "I'm afraid he's going to kill somebody when he's out there driving around out of his mind. I don't think my parents could handle that."

It is all too easy for families to fear the worst when they are trying to cope with addiction. The bizarre world of addiction makes almost any terrible event seem possible and even likely. Families learn to fear the ringing of the telephone or an unexpected knock on the door. They become afraid when they haven't heard from the addict in a while and, if the addict has episodes of anger or violence, are even more afraid when the addict shows up at their door.

The fear that springs from the family's love and concern for the addict becomes one of the addict's favorite weapons in the game of manipulation. It is very hard to say no to somebody when you fear the consequence might be that person's death. It is hard to stand your ground when you fear that your loved one will end up behind bars or living on the streets.

Jerry and Teresa, whose daughter had become addicted to prescription drugs, described a scene in which they tried to force her to check into a residential treatment program. The daughter, who was living in their home at the time, insisted she wasn't ready. Teresa recalled: "Feelings escalated and she was crying, and finally she started throwing her clothes into a black garbage bag. She said she couldn't take the pressure of living with us and was going to go check into this shelter that had a terrible reputation. It took in the lowest of the low, the hard-core addicts. There were constant fights and stealing, twelve or fifteen people to a room, people on blankets on the floor. The thought of it terrified me. So anyway, she threw her bag over her shoulder and said that's where she was going, and my heart just broke. I couldn't stand the thought of my little girl in that place. I started crying, and the next thing I knew, I was begging her to stay. She didn't have to go into a program if she wasn't ready. I backed down completely."

Teresa said that, looking back on the incident, she can see that she was manipulated. But all she felt at the time was fear for her daughter's safety. That's why she let her daughter stay home and continue to use drugs.

Guilt is another favorite manipulative tool of addicts. Addicts commonly try to find someone to blame for their situation, and that someone is frequently a parent, spouse, or other family member.

Most parents, when looking back on how they raised their children, have at least some regrets. They may wish that they had been more or less strict, that they had expected more or less of their children, that they had spent more time with them, or that they had not been so overprotective. They may reflect on difficult events, such as a divorce or death in the family, and see these as turning points in their child's mental health. Some may bear heavy burdens of shame over past difficulties, such as an infidelity that damaged the family and caused mistrust. Whatever the parental failings may be, it is almost inevitable that the addicts will recognize these vulnerable spots and take advantage of the parents. Here's an example of how it works.

Judy's first husband was an alcoholic who abused her and terrorized the children when he was drunk. Because they had been high school sweethearts and she loved him and kept hoping he'd change, she stuck by him for nearly ten years before getting a divorce. Twenty years later, her oldest son, then twenty-eight, became a heroin addict. Judy was devastated and consumed with guilt. If only she'd left her husband sooner, if only her child hadn't witnessed the violence, if only he hadn't lived with so much chaos, he would never have turned to drugs. His addiction was her fault. This was what she told herself. It was also what her son told her. Whenever

Judy brought up the subject of his addiction, whenever she urged him to seek help or refused to "loan" him money, he countered with the bitter reminder that it was all her fault. Her guilt would resurface, and she would drop the subject or give him what he asked for.

In an effort to manipulate, addicts are apt to tell their parents such things as "You didn't love me enough" or "Nothing I ever did was good enough for you" or "You were never the father I needed you to be." One young woman angrily told her parents, "You never listened to what I wanted. You forced me to take dancing lessons even though I hated them." Another, the child of an alcoholic mother, told her older sister, "You abandoned me when you went to college. If you'd cared about me, you wouldn't have left me with Mom."

Between spouses, the guilt game may take a slightly different twist. Addicts may try to induce guilt by singling out personal "flaws" as well as past behaviors. They say such things as "I wouldn't have to drink so much if you could keep these kids under control" or "I wouldn't have to use drugs if you were more fun (or good-looking or sexy or interesting or rich)." This type of finger-pointing usually has no validity, but spouses often feel a guilty sense of responsibility for the addicts' problems nonetheless.

Addicts may have many complaints, including major and minor grievances from years past. Some of their accusations may, in fact, have truth in them. Families may well have caused pain for the addicts. They may well have failed the addicts in some significant way. (After all, what human relationship is perfect?) But addicts bring up these problems not to clear the air or with the hope of healing old wounds. They bring them up solely to induce guilt, a tool with which they manipulate others in pursuit of their continued addiction.

Another common manipulative tool is pity. Addicts are, in

general, pitiful people. Many of them struggle with depression. For those in treatment, a dual diagnosis of depression and addiction is not uncommon, although it is sometimes difficult to determine whether or not the depression stems from addiction. Many of them suffer from social alienation, shattered relationships, and loneliness. Most are burdened with overwhelming problems such as bad credit, debt, and marginal employability. The difficulties resulting from addiction can be truly momentous, arousing a great deal of concern and pity in those who love the addict.

Most addicts are not averse to using this pity to their own advantage, as Doreen and Jake's story illustrates. Doreen, a heavyset woman in her late fifties, worked in a nursing home as a nurse's aide. It was a physically grueling job, requiring her to lift patients, make beds, change diapers, empty bedpans, and provide general care for ten or more elderly patients every day. Doreen suffered from chronic back pain and a bad knee, but she worked all the overtime she could get in order to support herself and Jake, her thirty-eight-year-old son. Jake had been an alcoholic since his midteens. He had lived independently in his early twenties, but after several failed relationships, he moved in with his mother. Once there, he seemed to require more and more care. Doreen worried about his health, so she cooked a nutritious meal for him every day. She worried about his lack of grooming, so she did his laundry and forced him to shower and even cut his hair when he had no money for the barber. She worried about his general aimlessness and lack of motivation, so she drove him to his counseling appointments and to job interviews.

Sometimes Doreen felt resentful and threatened to throw him out. Then he would say something such as "I don't blame you, Ma. No one would want me," and pity would make her relent. One day he took her car without permission (as he often did) and got into a serious accident. One of his legs was permanently damaged. He took to lying in bed or on the couch for hours on end, smoking cigarettes and watching television. The only time he was motivated to move was when he ran out of alcohol, at which point he would hobble to the corner store. Doreen suggested that if he was healthy enough to get alcohol, he should be healthy enough to get a job and move out. But he said, "You're so hard, Ma. I need something for the pain. Besides, where would I go? No one wants an old cripple like me." Again, pity made her back off, and her son got exactly what he wanted: a comfortable home in which to indulge his addiction.

Not all addicts are as overt in their bids for pity. Some arouse pity merely by the circumstances of their lives, such as the heroin addict who has been evicted from his apartment and has no place to go or the crack addict whose skeletal appearance suggests imminent death. Families, taking pity, want to provide a home or buy groceries or otherwise take care of their pitiful loved ones. My own daughter, who often seemed depressed and listless, aroused so much pity in me that I bought her a car, thinking that would cheer her up. A month later, she and her boyfriend were living in the car, so I let her move into my house. There, I reasoned, she would be free to focus on her recovery.

Three cars and several thousand dollars later, I realized that buying cars for her was not the answer to her problems. Neither, perhaps, was letting her live with me. She continued to use heroin despite her promises not to, and whenever I approached the subject, she would either react with anger (which she soon discovered did not work to her advantage) or with tears (which often worked). She would say that she was trying, but that she was so lonely, that she had no friends, and that her life was pointless and empty. The topic of conversation would then shift from her addiction and what she was doing about it to her pervasive sadness. I believe that the sadness was genuine, but I eventually came to see that when my pity kicked in, she gained the upper hand in the conversation. The focus would shift from a topic that made her uncomfortable—namely, her addiction and what she was doing about it—to a more comfortable one of herself as a victim in a situation over which she had no control.

Because pity usually reinforces addicts' sense of helplessness, it can be very damaging in their search for recovery. But as a manipulative tool to enable them to continue using, it is very effective.

BEHAVIORS THAT ARE SYMPTOMATIC OF ADDICTION

In my experience, denial, dishonesty, and manipulation are the behaviors most fundamental to addiction. They are the behaviors addicts call on time and again in the all-consuming effort to get drugs, use drugs, and conceal the addiction from others. These behaviors become like second nature, helping the addiction take root and blossom.

However, there are other behaviors associated with addiction that are often more readily apparent and that make the experience of dealing with addicts confusing, even bizarre. These behaviors result from the effects of the alcohol or other drugs themselves. They include withdrawal from family and friends, defensiveness, lack of responsibility, lack of personal hygiene, and irrational and inexplicable mood swings.

My daughter exhibited all of these behaviors over a two-year time span. I kept trying to convince myself that she was suffering from nothing more serious than mild depression. She was living with her boyfriend in an apartment about a fifteen-minute walk from my house, yet I rarely saw her. She avoided answering the phone or opening the door when I rang her bell. Once she was coming out of her building just as I was arriving, and she became hysterical. "Why can't you leave me alone? Why are you always bothering me?" she cried. I had never seen her so frantic and had no idea at the time that she was coming down from a cocaine high.

On another occasion, after her phone was disconnected and neither her friends nor I had heard from her in more than a week, I became so alarmed that I asked her landlord to let me into her apartment. I had been ringing her bell and knocking on her door off and on for most of the day with no response. As he inserted the key, he banged on the door, and I called out her name yet again. There was no response, so he pushed the door open. I was convinced that she had moved away or was dead. Instead, as the door opened, my daughter and her boyfriend jumped up from their futon, not more than three feet from the door, with a surprised exclamation of "What the fuck!" Anger and accusations followed. "You're psychotic, Mom," she screamed. "Why can't you accept that I'm grown up? I don't have to be hanging out with my mother anymore."

The refusal to answer the door became a common thread throughout her addiction to cocaine and then to heroin, as did her reluctance to participate in family gatherings or join me in activities she had once enjoyed, such as going to the movies or going out to eat. She became increasingly isolated and treated every overture of kindness from her friends, her siblings, and me as an invasion of her privacy. Her rare inter-actions with the family usually resulted in scenes of hysteria or tears. Amazingly, through it all, I persisted in my own de-nial of her drug problems, although they were the obvious explanation of the terrible changes I was seeing in her.

Another mother told me of a similar experience with her

son, a thirty-two-year-old licensed electrician. "He used to be so responsible," she said. "He made good money and had some close friends, and I thought he was set for life. Oh, I knew he smoked pot, but I didn't consider it a problem. He had a good head on his shoulders. Then everything fell apart. He stopped paying his rent. He wrecked his truck and lost his job. His phone and electricity were shut off, and he stopped coming around to visit. We all saw him less and less. Looking back, there were plenty of red flags, but I didn't see them.

"Finally he admitted to his brother that he was hooked on heroin. When I learned the truth, I went over there and banged on his door for at least an hour. I was screaming his name at the top of my lungs. The neighbors must have thought I was a crazy woman. Finally, I said I was going to get the cops to break down the door because I really thought he must be dead in there. What else could I think? That's when he opened the door. He looked awful, thin and sickly. He let me in, but he turned his back to me. He kept saying he just wanted to be left alone. Why couldn't I just leave him alone? I started yelling at him. I couldn't help myself. I kept asking how he could he be so stupid, things like that. I was out of my mind. After a while, I don't know how long, he just broke down and sobbed. He was like a little boy."

Her anger at her son's "stupidity" was mingled with disbelief. "It was like a nightmare," she recalled. How could drug addiction change her son from the clear-headed, hardworking young man she had always known into the irresponsible, emotional wreck she saw before her? It seemed impossible that this weeping, fragile man was truly her son.

Yet the kind of transformation she witnessed in her son is one that is seen all too often by families who are struggling with addiction. Families try desperately to say the right word or do the right thing that will snap their addict out of the insane behavior. They try reasoning, threatening, or any tactic that may formerly have affected the addict's actions. But their efforts are usually futile—for the simple reason that the addict's brain has been dramatically altered by addiction.

Scientists are only recently exploring the ways that addiction physically alters the brain. What is becoming increasingly clear is that giving up alcohol or other drugs is not a simple matter of choice or willpower. The addicted brain itself functions differently from a nonaddicted brain, and addiction affects every aspect of the addict's physical and emotional existence.

This knowledge is terrifying for most families, driving home the point of just how appalling their loved one's condition is. But there is also strength in knowledge. No addiction is hopeless, and by understanding how addiction works, families can find effective strategies for coping with this terrible disease.

THREE

THE BEAST INSIDE

John, a recovering crack addict whose grown children were fighting their own battles with addiction, described how hard quitting for good had been for him thirteen years earlier: "Their mother, my wife, had walked out on us, and I knew I was in danger of losing my kids if I didn't get clean. I was scared and motivated to stop using. I can't tell you how many times I'd get off work and tell myself, 'I'm not going to use. I'm not going to use.' Then I'd call my dealer and drive over to his house thinking, 'I'm not going to use.' I'd give him the money for the stuff, cook it up, and put it in the pipe, all the time telling myself, 'I'm not going to use.' Then I'd light it up, smoke it, and say, 'Damn! I used again.'"

As John explained it, when he started getting serious about getting clean, he often felt like two people: the good father who wanted to do right by his kids and the addict who cared only about getting high. According to him, "It was almost as if there was this other person living inside me, this crazy person who I couldn't control."

My daughter described a similar feeling one night, crying, "Sometimes I feel like there's a beast inside me."

Whether it's a beast inside or a monkey on the back,

addiction has the power to wipe out reason, willpower, and good intentions. It creates a perverted reality within addicts' minds in which obsession with the addictive substance obliterates the capacity for rational thought. This condition is not a figment of their imagination. Addiction works by actually altering normal brain functioning.

In its simplest terms, addiction can be viewed as a combination of two circumstances: *physical dependence,* or tolerance, which may, but does not necessarily, produce withdrawal symptoms, and *obsessive thinking,* which causes the addict's life to revolve around the use of alcohol or other drugs.

No one sets out to become an addict. No one decides one day, "I guess I'll use this drug until I become addicted, and then I'll just go ahead and alienate everybody I know and lose everything of value." Instead, addiction begins deep within the brain with physical and chemical changes to the systems that process information. Of particular significance is the way that addiction changes the experience of pleasure.

We are all born with the capacity to feel pleasure. From a strictly biological perspective, pleasure is a survival mechanism. Food and sex can trigger intense feelings of pleasure, and both are fundamental to our survival as a species. Other pleasurable experiences, including satisfying relationships, personal accomplishments, and the appreciation of natural or artistic beauty, add meaning and purpose to life.

We can all name specific experiences that produce sensations of pleasure and describe what those sensations *feel* like. But scientists can go even further. They can identify the electrical and chemical activities that occur within the brain to generate those good sensations.

THE BIOLOGY OF ADDICTION

The brain contains billions of impulse-conducting cells called neurons. These neurons, or nerve cells, have an axon that transmits impulses away from a cell to dendrites that help conduct impulses to another cell.

Neurons communicate with each other by releasing chemical messengers, or neurotransmitters, across tiny spaces called synapses. Many neurotransmitters then normally return to the dendrite to be reused again and again. Dendrites contain special receptor sites to receive specific neurotransmitters, just as a lock is designed to accommodate a specific key. There may be as many as three hundred different types of neurotransmitters within the brain, each carrying an individual message for pleasure, pain, fear, anger, and so on.

Our experience of pleasure occurs primarily within two central gray areas of the brain, the nucleus accumbens and the ventral tegmentum. These so-called pleasure centers are closely connected to the brain's system for processing appetite, sex, pain, memory, and emotions. The network within the pleasure centers, known as the pleasure or reward circuit, is highly receptive to the neurotransmitter dopamine, the pleasure messenger. Dopamine is released when the pleasure circuit is stimulated by enjoyable activities such as eating a delicious meal or listening to good music.

Addictive substances also stimulate the reward circuit, artificially inducing powerful sensations of pleasure. Although the mechanics vary from drug to drug, most addictive substances target the reward circuit and generate an intense concentration of dopamine. (Heroin also stimulates the release of endorphins, opiatelike neurotransmitters that promote pleasure and reduce pain and stress.) The result is a feeling of euphoria, a "rush" or "high" so powerful that addicted laboratory rats will ignore food and work themselves to death to obtain drugs.

Unfortunately for addicts, the feeling of intense pleasure is only a temporary consequence of repeated use. A more lasting—and damaging—consequence is that the number of dopamine receptors may be reduced as the brain attempts to regain its equilibrium. Research suggests that the more an addictive substance is used, the more dopamine receptors are destroyed. If the dopamine cannot connect with a receptor, it cannot deliver the pleasure message. As a result, a "hit" that used to deliver a high can no longer do so, and a user must increase the dose of the addictive substance in order to achieve the same effects. Thus tolerance and the need for increasing amounts of drugs develop.

Lia, a twenty-two-year-old recovering heroin addict, explained tolerance by saying, "I know it sounds weird, but when you're physically addicted, you need it so you won't get sick. You need it to feel normal. You don't get high. You feel relaxed, numb, kind of happy."

But the desire to feel "normal" is not what propels addiction along its disastrous course. Rather, addiction is fueled by the irresistible compulsion to experience again and again the rush of pleasure—the high. To achieve this, addicts must either be clean for a period to lower their tolerance level (some addicts go in and out of rehab for this very reason) or continually increase their alcohol or other drug intake.

Jane, a mother of two whose heroin addiction led to the loss of her children, multiple prison sentences, and life on the streets, described her need for ever-larger amounts of drugs: "So I leave the prerelease [from prison] and get an apartment. My mother had had my kids for three years at that point. They'd come out on weekends. Then I started scheduling the kids one weekend and go get high on the other weekend. I thought, 'I can do this so no one knows.' Then my boyfriend gets out of jail, and we start shooting a lot of dope. Every time I had my kids, my mother would give me money. So now it was about getting the money, getting the kids to get the money. The kids stayed all summer. I lost my apartment and ended up moving into what's called a squatter. There were still some tenants in the building, but it was mostly abandoned. And I was running around all day with my boyfriend getting high, and I'd send my kids to the Boys and Girls Club and they would feed them, and I would feed them cereal or macaroni and cheese at night. My boyfriend got nine hundred dollars a month in disability, and we'd spend it in a day."

Mark, a married father of two who often worked two jobs to support his family during many years of active alcoholism, described his experience with the progression of the disease: "It was a very slight downhill slope. When I got married, I was drinking two or three beers a day and drinking all day and into the evening on weekends. Then I started going out for noon beers, especially on Fridays. Then it turned into Thursdays, Wednesdays, every day. I was drinking three-quarters of a case a beer a day, maybe more, and three or four shots of whiskey. I wouldn't feel so good when I woke up, so one day I had a couple of shots or beers to straighten me out in the morning. It worked, so I did it again, and it turned into three or four or as many as I could get before I got into the shop. At the end, the drinking was continual."

Not only do addicts find it increasingly difficult to experience the pleasurable effects of early substance use, their brains also lose receptivity to the normal pleasures of food, beauty, companionship, and sex. Those ordinary pleasures fail to stimulate the brain, which has been conditioned to the intensity of drug highs. Studies of dogs that had their reward circuits artificially stimulated confirmed that the loss of normal pleasure is not just a perception but a physical phenomenon. The dogs' brains released great amounts of dopamine in response to artificial stimulation, but when the dogs were given juicy meat bones, their brains released no dopamine at all. This helps to explain why most addicts eventually lose interest in people and activities that once brought them pleasure. To the addicted brain, the chemical high becomes not only an intense source of pleasure, but also the *only* source of pleasure.

As Jane explained it, losing her children, her home, her job, and her freedom were not enough to make her stop using drugs, because none of those things brought her the pleasure that drugs did. She said, "I loved shooting dope. It made me feel good. It was what I lived for."

Further deepening the process of addiction is the flip side of pleasure: pain. Sigmund Freud speculated that "our entire psychological activity is bent upon producing pleasure and avoiding pain." Certainly addicts suffer both psychological and physical pain as a consequence of their addiction. When deprived of its customary drugs, the chemically dependent brain experiences an onslaught of stressful responses, such as fear, anxiety, panic, and severe depression. Withdrawal can also produce physiological symptoms that range from persistent discomfort to intense pain. Withdrawal can also cause seizures, strokes, even death. Addicts describe periods of drug deprivation with such phrases as "I was crawling out of my skin" or "I had the shakes so bad I couldn't walk."

The addicted brain, when in distress, craves the drug that has consistently provided relief from pain. In this way, positive reinforcement (pleasure) combines with negative reinforcement (relief from pain) to tighten the grip of addiction.

Of course, the human brain functions as much more than

a vehicle to process pleasure and pain. It is, in fact, our primary survival tool. Our brain and its miraculous ability to reason, assess situations, solve problems, and predict consequences enabled us to become the dominant species on the planet. Without our incredible brains, we physically vulnerable humans may well have become just another failed evolutionary experiment.

Unfortunately, addiction short-circuits higher mental functions by concentrating the brain's energy on the obsessive pursuit of pleasure. In his book *The Selfish Brain,* former U.S. Drug Czar Robert L. DuPont, M.D., says:

> Addiction is a perversion of brain biology . . . because, unlike feeding, aggression, and sex, there is no biological purpose to the use of addicting drugs. Addiction is brain stimulation devoid of biological meaning. (p. 230)

THE PSYCHOLOGY OF ADDICTION

Anyone who has witnessed the downward spiral of an addict's life has been frustrated and bewildered by the addict's repetitive pattern of poor choices and disastrous consequences. As we have seen, biology is partly to blame because psychoactive substances dramatically alter brain functioning. Less understood is the psychological imperative behind addiction. Like certain forms of mental illness, addiction is a disease that consistently tells the victim there is nothing wrong. The addict's life may be falling to pieces, everything of value may be slipping away, but the addicted brain says such reassuring things as "You're okay" or "You can handle this" or "You don't have a problem—*they* do."

To make matters worse, these twisted perceptions are validated by substance-generated feelings of intense pleasure—a perverse fusion of false perceptions and biological reinforcement. (Similarly, anorexics, who perceive that they are overweight even when they are dying of starvation, experience increased levels of endorphins, the brain's natural opiates, when they don't eat.)

To begin understanding the psychological basis of addiction, we must first recognize that addiction is fundamentally obsessive-compulsive in nature. Obsessive-compulsive disorder in the general population is a mental condition that causes persistent unwelcome thoughts and images accompanied by the irresistible urge to perform repetitive actions or rituals. It is an anxiety disorder thought to originate in unresolved internal conflict. This serious condition can interfere with a person's ability to live a normal life, and many who suffer from it can recover only with the help of psychotherapy and sometimes medication.

In addicts, powerful obsessive-compulsive urges center on obtaining, preparing, and using alcohol or other drugs. Like others afflicted with this condition, addicts are unable to control their thoughts, and they feel compelled to use again and again, despite severe consequences that often result from their actions.

As Lia explained it, "When I was an active addict, drugs were the only thing I thought about from the moment I started to wake up to the time I went to sleep. I even dreamed about them. I couldn't escape thinking about drugs, and the thoughts were so huge there wasn't room for anything else."

The urge to use takes on a psychological life of its own, making relapse a prevalent problem among the addicted population. Being clean, even for extended periods, and allowing the brain to return to normal biological functioning sometimes does little to prevent the obsessive thinking and compulsive urges that can lead recovering addicts to resume their use of alcohol or other drugs.

The obsessive-compulsive nature of addiction extends beyond the substance itself to encompass people, places, and paraphernalia—everything associated with the process of getting high. Crack addicts can experience pleasure just by looking at their blackened fingers. A heroin addict wrote, "I love the low-down, dirty lifestyle that goes along with being a junkie. I love sticking needles in my arms. I admire the bubbly, red blood when it trickles into the syringe." Another addict explained, "You sort of get addicted to the whole drug lifestyle, the process of getting drugs, how you get high, whom you get high with, what you do for money. It's so baffling, but it's more than the drugs. It's the whole process, preparing the needle, hearing the whoosh when it sucks up the drugs, cooking coke on the stove, shooting it into your arms, all of that. I love the way the needle feels."

Psychologically, these feelings can be explained by the phenomenon of association. Most of us are familiar with Ivan Pavlov's famous experiment in which he conditioned dogs to salivate when a bell was rung. The dogs associated the bell with food, and the ringing triggered the expectation of pleasure. Similarly, addicts associate sets of experiences with pleasure. They can find enjoyment in apparently appalling situations because those situations are associated with the rewarding experience of the substance-induced high.

The psychological process of association is also responsible for two common aspects of addiction: triggers and cravings. As applied to addiction, a trigger is a mental cue that produces thoughts about a particular substance or experience. Triggers may be sensory (sights, sounds, smells, and so on), verbal (a word or phrase that is somehow associated

with the substance), or emotional. A craving is an overwhelming desire for that substance or experience.

Triggers and cravings are common to the human experience, as anyone who has ever been on a diet knows. Seeing a
food commercial on television, smelling certain odors, even
driving past a favorite restaurant can weaken our resolve to
eat less. I was once traveling with a friend who had a weak-
ness for sweets. As we passed an A&W root beer stand, he
commented that A&W made the best root beer floats in the
world. I suggested that we stop so he could buy one, but
he declined. He was "watching his weight." Forty or so miles
later, as night was falling, he said he recalled passing a motel a
few miles back. We turned around and eventually found ourselves at the A&W stand, where he ordered a large float. The
thought of that float had been working on his mind for more
than an hour and had finally proven irresistible.

Triggers seem to be a feature of human psychology from
an early age, as we can see from the effectiveness of advertis-
ing that targets children. When children enter a store, they
are drawn to food, toys, and other items they have seen in
commercials because they have been conditioned to associate
those items with pleasure. When the Scooby-Doo movie was
released in 2002, my three-year-old grandson excitedly
pointed out every promotional poster and billboard we
passed, things I would not have noticed if he hadn't been with
me. Evidently, he associated Scooby-Doo with fun—with
pleasure.

Triggers evoke stored memories of special meaning. What
triggers a reaction or a craving in one person may be completely meaningless to another. When I bought my daughter a
pair of sneakers early in her recovery, she pointed out that
the slogan on the box read "Get the addiction," a phrase I had
overlooked. She also asked me about a cardboard box on my

closet shelf that was printed with images of syringes. The box had come from a clinic where one of my other children had worked, and it contained an old china tea set. I had never noticed the images before because they had no meaning for me.

The difficulty for addicts is that triggers can be almost anything, and the resulting cravings can be particularly intense. Places and people associated with getting high are obvious triggers. However, most are not so easily predictable.

One addict described hearing a siren one day, which reminded him of the ringing sensation in his head that had often accompanied the rush of cocaine. "It was a head rush, like an electric shock through my whole body," he said. "All of a sudden I just wanted it so bad."

An alcoholic described her feelings when passing a liquor store or seeing a beer commercial: "You get weak. You can taste it. You want it so bad it's unreal."

Another addict recalled seeing a stranger who was wearing a blue blouse. She said, "My mind went from the color blue to my old jean jacket to shooting up in about half a second, and I was soon thinking, 'Okay—I'm gonna go out and cop, and I'm gonna do this and that' all in a second. Your mind just goes there."

Another addict recalled watching a Fourth of July parade from the porch of a halfway house. She said, "One of the marchers had a mustache like a guy I used to get high with. I started to shake. I had to go inside before I went out and scored some dope."

Emotions, sometimes barely perceived, can trigger intense cravings. The mind senses boredom, loneliness, guilt, fear, anxiety, or other unpleasant feelings and, for substance abusers, instantly identifies the remedy as alcohol or other drugs. For the nonaddicted, food, television, or other substances or activities are the "solution."

Jane described a painful breakup of an important relationship by saying, "There was this lump in my throat, like my heart was in my throat. I knew that if I did a bag of dope, the lump would go away."

Ironically, happy feelings can also trigger cravings because the greedy brain wants to intensify the good feelings. The logic might go something like this: "I feel good now, and by smoking a little dope, I'll feel even better." It's the same thinking that causes many people to eat to excess: "One cookie makes me feel good. If I eat a dozen, I'll feel even better." The brain selectively forgets the negative feelings that usually result from binges and recalls only the immediate reward.

Triggers and cravings, conditioned responses that stem from the psychological phenomenon of association, are common to all human beings. But association is not the only influence that psychology has on addiction. Another major influence is "self-talk": the messages that addicts, like all people, tell themselves.

A well-established view of the human experience is that most of us live up or down to our own self-image. That is, our beliefs about ourselves play a tremendous role in determining our path in life. If we believe we are deserving and capable, we are likely to make choices and take chances that may promote our well-being. If we believe we are not worthy or that we never have any luck, we are likely to make choices that will fulfill those beliefs. Addicts are not exempt from this principle. Their self-talk and "stinking thinking" are apt to include messages that prolong and deepen their addiction.

Jane recalled some of her own self-talk during her period of deepest addiction: "I always believed in God, but I just thought God made all sorts of people. I was simply one of those people, a junkie that God made. That's what I thought. God said you will always be a drug addict. Because I loved shooting dope, that's what I lived for. I'd already given my kids up, and I accepted it."

Jane went on to describe the feeling of hopelessness that often accompanies addiction. According to her, "You get to a point when you're using where you say, 'Fuck it.' I looked at all the damage I had done and I thought, 'There's no way I can fix this.' I was shooting everything under the sun because I couldn't fix what I had damaged."

Jane added that she would act tough and tell people that she liked the way she was, but "inside I hated myself; I wanted to die." Lia recalled, "I always felt like shit." Mark said, "I was disgusting, and I knew it. But I couldn't change, so I drank even more." The messages that addicts tell themselves—that they can't fit into "normal" society, that they can't make it without a chemical crutch, that they're bad or weak or hopeless—are psychological whips that beat down their spirits and make addiction all the more powerful.

THE RECKLESS PURSUIT OF PLEASURE

The biology and psychology of addiction combine to narrow the brain's focus to the meaningless pursuit of pleasure. As a result, the brain's ability to function in reasonable, life-enhancing, and lifesaving ways is diminished. The brain's considerable power becomes focused primarily on obtaining and using alcohol or other drugs. Skills such as paying bills, working at a career, building relationships, planning for the future, and taking care of one's physical health are lost. Furthermore, the addicted brain will push the addict into dangerous, life-threatening situations, such as engaging in stealing or prostitution or combing dangerous neighborhoods in search of drugs.

Mark recalled that at the height of his active alcoholism he was more than eighty pounds overweight, his eyes were always bloodshot, his sweat reeked of alcohol, and he felt sick to the point of exhaustion. Still, he could not stop drinking. Jane, who routinely turned tricks to support her habit, continued to solicit sex even when a serial killer was known to be murdering prostitutes in her town.

Lia, who followed a popular band's concert tours around the country, described having no fear in a number of perilous situations: "I've walked through every single ghetto across this country with acid in one pocket [to sell] and needles in another. I'd be scared about getting arrested so I'd be checking out for the cops, but I'd walk up to a crack house, a dope house, with my money on me. Sometimes when I bought drugs I'd try it right there, to make sure it's real. One time I woke up in a crack house where I didn't know anybody. But I really didn't have any fear.

"Sometimes when I was doing a lot of coke, I'd get a really big ringer. It's this kind of psychotic feeling, a loud siren whirring in your head. Your heart's racing, your head's spinning, your eyes are open, and you think, 'Oh my God, I'm going to die.' That's freaky because it's more of an awake thing. But with heroin, you don't get scared. You don't notice. You're really, really relaxed. It's more like, 'Okay, I'm going to die. Like, everybody dies.' Know what I mean?"

That the addicted brain loses its power to recognize danger became clear to me when my daughter described attending the funeral of a heroin addict who had died of an overdose. I asked if seeing the effects of heroin had frightened her into wanting to get clean. She calmly replied, "Mom, when addicts hear that someone has OD'd, they think, 'That must have been good stuff. Where can I get some?'"

She also told me that her boyfriend had OD'd several times, and she described one scene in some detail: "We had just shot up, and I was nodding on the couch. For some reason I opened my eyes, and I saw him facedown on the floor. I called 911. They came, gave him a shot, and took him to the emergency room. If I hadn't opened my eyes, he would have died."

Another addict, who OD'd many times, described one such incident: "My friends had shot me full of saltwater, because that's supposed to bring you back, but it didn't. So they called 911. The EMTs were working on me when I came to. I thought, 'No, no.' They were wrecking my high, and I wanted them to leave me alone. They took me to the hospital anyway. I was so high I gave them my home address, so my mom got the emergency room bill. Usually I would've given a fake address."

Those experiences didn't stop any of these addicts from continuing their drug use. Their addicted brains had ceased to be tools for survival and had become instruments of pleasure—at any cost.

Ironically, as addiction progresses and the meaning of life is reduced to the reckless pursuit of pleasure, an addict's life almost invariably becomes one of unremitting misery. Problems multiply, losses mount, and the physical, emotional, and spiritual toll becomes enormous. The trouble starts with a pleasurable high that grows more and more elusive. Then the pursuit of the high makes addicts become all the more desperate. Other interests and obligations—personal values, family, friends, job, bills—fall to the bottom of the priority list, and the addicts begin to suffer in unimaginable ways.

"I could clear a room just by walking into it," Mark recalled. "Nobody wanted to be around me."

Jane remembered living with her children in "a cute little house that was only sixty dollars a month" and being evicted for not paying rent because all her money was going for drugs. She also remembered how drugs changed her relationship with her boyfriend: "When we were first together, he didn't want me working the streets. He didn't like that. At the end, he'd tell me to go out and make some money."

Most painful to Jane is remembering the effect her addiction had on her children, who spent most of their childhood with her mother. She recalled, "I started mixing heroin and cocaine. It was totally awesome, and I loved it. So for two years I'm a maintenance heroin addict, doing two bags a day. Then I meet this guy who shows me how to steal. He'd go into a store and steal, and I'd bring it back for cash. Now I'm shooting ten bags a day, and my kids are starting to interfere because I have to feed them, bathe them, and stop and let them play. One day I left them with a baby-sitter, packed up my whole house into a U-Haul, and took off for Florida with my boyfriend."

Jane devoted most of the next six years to doing drugs, with frequent stints in jail and halfway houses. Occasionally pangs of guilt reached her conscience, but even this couldn't make her stop: "So now I'm living with the guilt of leaving my kids. I thought about them all the time. One time when my son's birthday came up, I was sitting in a shooting gallery saying, 'Today is my son's birthday. Today is the most important day in my life, when I gave birth to this human being.' I'd remember all that and I'd sob and sob, then shoot more dope. I'd become a crazy person. I jumped through a window, took a knife and slit my throat. I wanted to kill myself. I kept saying, 'How could I do this to my kids?' But I couldn't stop."

Lia, too, suffered deeply because of her addiction. She said: "One time I was in this halfway house and people were talking about prostitution, and I could not even envision it. Never in my wildest dreams. No way in hell. You know what I mean? It just was not in my vision. I couldn't picture how that could happen, because when I was dope sick before, that would never even enter my mind. The first thing I would think about was stealing, conning, or manipulating, getting money somehow, but I wouldn't do that. That's the scary part, because it was unreal to me. But it kind of just happened.

"I was dope sick and really needed money, and I just started doing it. You're numb; there's no feeling at all. I didn't even care. I'd tell myself, 'I'm getting money for it. There's nothing romantic about this. It's just a job.'

"The more I did it, the more I had to use. I was shooting heroin and cocaine all the time. My head was always hanging down when I was with my real friends. I felt numb. One day my boyfriend and I got in this huge fight. He wasn't making any money. I was supplying the money and the drugs. Before he went to sleep he told me to save him some dope, but I used it all, so he flushed my needles down the toilet. We were screaming at each other, and we each had a champagne bottle in our hands, ready to hit each other. We just stopped and sort of gasped 'Oh my God' and started to cry. I looked around our house, with pizza boxes in one corner, ashes in another, a TV on cardboard boxes, spoons and needles in the kitchen, crack on the stove.

"That was a moment of clarity for me. I didn't want to live like that anymore, always fighting over money and drugs. In the beginning our relationship wasn't about drugs."

Broken relationships, poor health, destitution, and emotional and spiritual bankruptcy are the terrible price that most addicts eventually pay for their fleeting moments of pleasure.

WHO BECOMES ADDICTED?

To the average nonaddict, the thought of addiction holds an element of horror. What could be worse than losing your *self,* giving your mind over to the power of a perverting substance?

Even those of us who feel deep sympathy and compassion for an addict are apt to wonder how this could happen. After all, plenty of people use alcohol, marijuana, or even cocaine "recreationally" without becoming addicted. What is it about certain people that makes it impossible for them to use chemicals without getting hooked?

Many addicts, especially those who have examined their condition from the vantage point of recovery, express the belief that they were born addicts. They say that the seeds of addiction lay dormant within them, waiting only for the right conditions to trigger a full flowering of the disease.

"I was always an alcoholic and addict—always—and the painkillers triggered the addiction," said one man whose twin knee operations precipitated more than ten years of drug addiction.

Some addicts explain their condition as an "allergy" to substances of abuse. That is, some believe that psychoactive substances trigger a physiological reaction within their brains that is fundamentally different from the reaction of "non-allergic" people. While everyone will experience the physical high of the substance, the high seems special for the addict. It is more powerful, more meaningful, and more profound. Certainly, many addicts quickly develop an emotional connection to their substance of choice. They are apt to use the language of lovers when describing it: "It was what I was waiting for my whole life." "It was what I'd always been looking for." "Oh my God, I was in my glory." "I couldn't get enough of it."

Such powerful responses, while not clearly the result of an allergic reaction, may indeed be related to biological and environmental differences between those who become addicts and those who don't. Medical and social research strongly suggests that some people are genetically prone to addiction. The physiological basis for this tendency, the "addiction gene," has not been identified. But addiction does run in families, and research clearly shows that the children of addicts are at an increased risk of becoming addicts themselves. This does not mean that addiction is inherited. It does suggest that the vulnerability to addiction can be passed from one generation to the next.

Jane said that she grew up in a home where alcohol and other drugs were never present. She could find no genetic basis for her condition until she learned as an adult that the father who had raised her was not her biological father. "I was going through my mother's stuff and found some photographs of my mother with another man," she said. "She told me she divorced him because he was an abusive alcoholic. After that, he just kind of disappeared into the street life. I look just like him and probably inherited the addiction gene from him."

In my daughter's case, the genetic vulnerability to addiction was inherited from both parents. Her father is an alcoholic, her father's sister was a heroin addict, her paternal grandmother was addicted to "pep pills," and her paternal grandfather was an alcoholic (as were all his brothers). Her mother's sister was addicted to amphetamines, her maternal grandfather and both great-grandfathers were alcoholics, and one of her maternal great-grandmothers was addicted to codeine, an opium derivative.

Certainly, part of my daughter's genetic inheritance includes a tendency toward addiction. This does not excuse her, however, from taking responsibility for her addiction and recovery. It merely illustrates the point that the vulnerability to addiction can be passed through families much as the vulnerability to certain cancers or heart disease can pass from generation to generation.

Addiction is also widespread among individuals who suffer from mental illness. The National Co-Morbidity Survey conducted in the early 1990s indicates that there are about ten million adults in this country who suffer from at least one substance abuse disorder and at least one mental health disorder. According to the survey, the mental disorder developed first in 85 percent of these people.

Bert Pepper, M.D., a public health physician and psychiatrist who serves on the advisory board of the nation's Substance Abuse and Mental Health Services Administration (SAMHSA), noted in an interview:

> More than 60 percent of people with bipolar disorder have drug and/or alcohol problems, and the percentage for people with schizophrenia is even higher. And although the fifty-year-old alcoholic may have become addicted as a result of too many liquid lunches, 60 percent or more of young adult addiction patients have preexisting emotional, family, or psychiatric problems. So many adolescents have emotional needs that don't get attended to, and so they self-medicate.

In *Blamed and Ashamed,* a report published in 2001 by the Federation of Families for Children's Mental Health, Dr. Pepper writes:

> There are individuals who have no mental health problem and who become involved with the use of alcohol and drugs because they want to change the way they feel. These single-disorder individuals start out feeling okay but want to feel even better. Then substance abuse and addiction can make them feel much worse. But for depressed, anxious, shy, fearful, or hyperactive children

and adolescents, the motivation for drug use is very different. They are trying to just feel normal. (p. 49)

Individuals with co-occurring disorders, or dual diagnosis, frequently exhibit a number of immature behaviors because, in the words of Dr. Pepper:

The early development of anxiety, depression, thinking problems, and behavior problems, when compounded by the early use of drugs and alcohol, interferes with the development of a mature, stable, functional personality and sense of self. (p. 50)

He identifies behaviors that are typical of people with co-occurring disorders as follows: low frustration tolerance, lying to avoid punishment, hostile dependency (exhibiting hostility toward those whose help they rely on), limit-testing (normal in children but problematic in later adolescence and adulthood), alexithymia (the inability to verbalize feelings or ask for help), rejection sensitivity (an extreme need to be accepted), dualistic thinking (judging people and events as only right or wrong, good or bad, without accepting moderation or shades of gray), and present-tense thinking (lacking a sense of past or future, leading to repetition of the same mistakes over and over again).

Most of the parents I have spoken with about their child's addiction support these findings. Most say their child was depressed, anxious, or oversensitive before the substance abuse began. My own daughter certainly falls into this category. I remember asking a counselor early in my daughter's rehabilitation why some people get addicted while others don't. She said that, while there is no definitive answer, "Parents often remember that there was something just a

little different, a little out-of-step about the child even before the addiction began." (Dealing with co-occurring disorders presents special challenges for families and for those
in the treatment community. We will look at this topic more
closely in chapter 6.)

Similar to the problem of co-occurring disorders is a condition described by Dr. DuPont as "character disorder," which
is a blend of personality traits that puts certain individuals at
high risk of becoming addicts. In *The Selfish Brain,* he writes:

> The most prominent features of character disorder are
> thinking about the present rather than the future and
> frequent dishonesty. Other features include relative
> insensitivity to the feelings of others, rebellion against
> authority, and relative imperviousness to punishment.
> (p. 224)

The personal histories of many addicts support his observations. One twenty-one-year-old alcoholic recalled, "I was
this rebellious kid right from the beginning. I was always getting grounded. I was bad in school. I didn't get good grades. I
was always a risk-taker. I mean, at five years old I would jump
off anything. I'd jump into the biggest waves at the beach,
swim out deeper than anyone else. I can't remember ever
having fear. I think I was also an angry child. I don't know
what to blame it on, but there were times I was definitely
angry at my family. I don't really know why. I definitely had a
chip on my shoulder."

A twenty-five-year-old heroin addict said, "I was always
lying to my parents. One time when they thought I was going
to school, I got on a plane and flew two thousand miles away.
I did whatever I wanted, no matter what they did to me."

A forty-one-year-old addict and alcoholic remembered

running away from home when she was fourteen and dropping out of school at sixteen despite her parents' anger: "They were really hurt, but I didn't care. It didn't matter."

My own daughter was deceitful, rebellious, and stubborn— I thought of it as willful—even before she became addicted. For example, when she was twelve, I dropped her and a friend off at a neighborhood movie theater. Instead of going to the movie, they managed to buy cigarettes and smoked the entire pack even though it made them feel deathly ill. At fourteen she began to violate my privacy by wearing (and often ruining) my clothes and using my cosmetics and jewelry despite my repeated objections (a habit that continued well into her twenties). When she was fifteen, she stole one of my spare car keys and gave it to an older friend so they could drive around in my car without my knowledge whenever I was out for an evening.

Of course, rebelliousness, shortsightedness, and the desire to avoid consequences are typical traits of many teenagers and adults. Not everyone who exhibits character disorder becomes addicted. Nevertheless, most addicts do seem to have severe difficulty planning for the future, relating to the feelings of others, and learning from consequences. Addiction exacerbates these characteristics. It is also possible that character disorder is a manifestation of the mental or emotional illnesses that are so common among the addicted population.

In addition to genetics and mental health, environment plays a significant role in who does or does not become addicted. Home, community, and peer groups influence a person's attitude toward the use of mind-altering substances. If someone with a genetic vulnerability to addiction is part of a social group that strongly discourages the use of alcohol or other drugs, that person is less likely to try addictive substances than is a person with similar vulnerabilities who lives in an environment that tolerates the use of alcohol or other drugs.

When my children were growing up, alcohol was part of daily life. Alcohol was present at every meal except for breakfast. My husband and I drank alcohol every evening we were at home. Alcohol also figured prominently into every family gathering or holiday. I found nothing remarkable about any of this at the time. In hindsight, I see that my daughter learned early that chemical dependence is acceptable and even normal. (The fact that her brothers do not have a substance abuse problem suggests that they did not inherit the genetic tendency toward addiction.)

Although the attitudes and behaviors of family and peers help shape an individual's response to addictive substances, these are not the only influences. Another environmental consideration is availability. Quite simply, if a substance is not available, a person can't get hooked on it. For example, in the time and place where I grew up, alcohol was the only mind-altering chemical that was readily available. Marijuana was just beginning to be talked about, and LSD, cocaine, and heroin were almost unheard of. I knew of no one who had a drug problem. No one I knew had even tried marijuana. Now, of course, all that has changed. American teenagers from major cities to small towns have access to all the major addictive drugs, and drug-tolerant attitudes appear in movies, song lyrics, and television shows.

Age, too, plays a role in who becomes addicted. A number of studies have shown that people who begin experimenting with substances in their twenties may not become dependent until their fifties, if ever. However, someone who begins experimenting at sixteen may become dependent by twenty. And a child who begins using drugs, including nicotine, at ten or eleven may become dependent within just two years.

Although both genetics and environment play a role in addiction, which factor is predominant? The following examples lend some insight on this question.

During the Vietnam War, many in the U.S. service became addicted to heroin. For most of these people, their addiction was rooted in their environment. Heroin was plentiful, the normal rules of society didn't apply, and the stress of daily life created a stronger than usual desire for a chemical escape. Michael Hardiman writes in *Overcoming Addiction*:

> The establishment was concerned that, once the soldiers returned, American society would face a drug problem of unprecedented proportions. Despite all the dire predictions, something very different happened. Of the soldiers who were habitual heroin users, 92 percent stopped using the drug within one year of returning, most of them without any intervention. The remaining 8 percent was the same number of men who had used heroin before they joined the army. (p. 84)

It is reasonable to suppose that the individuals who were unable to stop their drug use had a biological vulnerability to addiction that was not present in those who were able to stop.

The influence of genetics and environment can also be seen in patients who become dependent on addictive pain medications. Although patients who are given certain medications for a longer period of time may become physically dependent on them, once the need for the pain medication is gone, most willingly stop using the drugs (although some require medical assistance to do so). In other words, once the environment that led to the drug use is altered, most patients no longer want to use the drugs. Patients who are genetically vulnerable to addiction, however, will want to continue taking the medication even after they no longer have a medical need for it and will, in fact, resist efforts to end the supply of drugs. For this reason, many substance abuse counselors advise their clients to avoid taking pain medications under all but the most dire circumstances.

CONFRONTING THE BEAST

The medical and scientific communities have made many advances in understanding addiction during the past decade or so. But many questions about the disease remain. Why, for example, do many addicts recover while some never do? Why do some addicts find recovery after only one rehabilitation experience while others enter rehab many times before recovery truly takes hold? And why do some addicts seek recovery after a relatively mild encounter with negative consequences while others suffer repeated traumatic losses and still continue their substance abuse?

The answers to these and other questions remain locked in the human psyche. What we do know is that addiction is a destructive, progressive disease that carries devastating consequences—both for addicts and for their families.

We also know that no one can cure an addict and that addicts must be fully responsible for finding and maintaining their own recovery. Nevertheless, families can have a positive influence on their addicted loved one, even if the addict does not live with or have much interaction with the family. They can do this by acting as role models for healthy living and by creating an environment that promotes recovery and personal growth. As a first step in creating a healthy, recovery-friendly environment, families must recognize and weed out their own unhealthy behaviors that have likely developed in response to their loved one's addiction.

FOUR

ADDICTED TO THE ADDICT

Celeste will never forget the moment she learned that her only son was addicted to heroin. His ex-girlfriend had hinted to her that he had a drug problem. Celeste was afraid to approach the question directly, and later when her son, a twenty-nine-year-old electrician, denied there was anything wrong, Celeste dropped the matter. But she herself had begun to observe some disturbing changes. When her son came to visit, he would flop on the couch as if he had no energy. Although he worked as hard as ever, he was usually short of money. He had lost weight, and his clothes no longer fit. He seemed listless and depressed.

After weeks of nagging, Celeste finally convinced her son to let her take him to a clinic for an evaluation. She recalled the events that followed: "A psychiatrist and a drug counselor met with each of us separately, then called us both in together. That's when the reality of the whole thing really hit me: he was using and had been for a long time. I was sitting in a room with these two people and my son, and all of this was coming out. I was shaking from head to toe. I couldn't control the shaking and felt absolutely in panic. It was as though I was just informed of the most horrible thing I could possibly imagine.

"My son was sitting there beside me, and they were trying to convince him that he needed to go into treatment. He was very defensive and kept saying he could do it on his own. At one point he reached over and grabbed my hand. It was clammy wet. The psychiatrist said to him, 'Look at her. Look what it's doing to her. She can't stop shaking.'

"Then the drug counselor said, 'He's not concerned right now about how you feel. All he cares about is how he's going to get his next fix. If he continues on this path, a year from now he will be in jail or dead.' She made it clear to me what shape my son was in. I couldn't comprehend the reality of what she was saying to me. I said, 'You don't understand, I'm just finding out about this tonight for the first time. I had no idea about what was going on.' I think I came close to passing out. It was as though my blood had been drained."

I experienced a similar sensation when I discovered that my daughter was a heroin addict. I had been worried about her for months, even years, as she lost jobs, got evicted from apartments, and became ever more reclusive. My fears came to a head one night as I drove past the apartment house where she had last been living. Her roommates had been threatening to throw her out, and I wondered if they actually had. I spotted her parked car on a side street and saw blankets, pillows, and some kitchen items piled in back. My heart began to race. She was almost certainly living in her car.

I later returned to the apartment house and leaned on the buzzer. "I want to find out what's happened to my daughter," I said through the intercom. Reluctantly, her roommates let me in. I could see that they were uncomfortable, maybe embarrassed. I asked if they knew where she was and why they had forced her to leave. They mumbled some words that didn't make much sense. I kept pressing for details, and finally one of them looked at me and said, "Do you know your daughter's a heroin addict?"

I remember grabbing a chair for support as the floor seemed to collapse under me. Everything became fuzzy and far away. I could barely breathe. "How do you know?" I asked.

I wanted proof. Although in shock, I didn't doubt the truth of what I had heard. The young woman before me was merely confirming what I had known and feared on some level for a long time. She went into details about my daughter, describing bloody tissues, nodding off at the kitchen table, and arms covered with scabs. I could barely take it in. I felt nauseated and terrified. Among the horrible images that crowded my mind, one thought rose to the top: I had to find my daughter and help her.

I returned to her car and waited on the dark street. After a long time, a white car pulled up, and my daughter emerged. The car was full of young men I didn't know. It drove away. I studied my daughter as she approached her car. She looked terrible. Her hair was matted flat to her head on one side, as if she had been sleeping. One of her heavily drawn-on eyebrows had worn off, giving her a lopsided look. She wore short shorts and a long-sleeved T-shirt.

I stepped out of the shadows and called her name. She gave me a sleepy, quizzical smile and asked what I was doing there. With a shaking voice I told her what I had learned. "Show me your arms," I demanded. She backed away. "Mom, you're psychotic! I haven't done anything wrong! You're psychotic!"

"Show me your arms!" I insisted.

She turned and bolted. I chased after her through narrow streets in a bad neighborhood that many women were afraid of even in daylight. "I'm never going to stop!" I called. "You're either coming home with me or we'll see a cop and I'll have you arrested! Those are your choices!" I felt strong saying that, believing I had taken charge of the situation. All her problems could be fixed now that I was taking matters into my own hands.

We ran for several blocks until she abruptly gave up and became quite passive. She returned willingly to my car. As I drove her home, we said little. I remember telling her to go to bed. We'd talk about things in the morning, I said, as if she were twelve years old. I thought I could come up with a solution overnight, and tomorrow everything would be all right.

I had no way of knowing the battle I was up against or the seriousness of my daughter's situation. Nor did I know that I was about to join millions of American families whose lives are made havoc by the disease of addiction.

It's true that the behavior of addicts' families often mirrors the disease of addiction itself. Just as addiction is characterized by denial, obsession with drugs, compulsion to use, and emotional and physical illness, family members experience denial, obsession with the addict, compulsion to control the addict, and emotional and physical illness. In a very real sense, families can become addicted to the addict. Like all addictions, the process begins with denial.

A GAME CALLED DENIAL

Most families, when describing their first encounters with a loved one's addiction, admit that they knew there was something wrong for a very long time. "All the signs were there, but we didn't want to see them," they say. "There were all these red flags that we didn't pay attention to." "I kept telling myself it wasn't possible, but I wasn't surprised when I found out."

A father recalled, "When I look back, there were a lot of little things. My son would stop by the house quite frequently and say, 'Dad, do you have five bucks I could borrow?' Everything in his house was so disorganized, so slovenly, and he was never like that. Everything used to be neat and organized, and his bills were paid on time. I remember telling myself he was depressed because his girlfriend had broken up with him."

One woman said that for more than a year she counted empty bottles in her mother's trash cans every time she went to visit. "When my husband would suggest that my mother had a drinking problem, I'd become furious with him. It was easier to pretend than to face the truth," she said.

A young man recalled that his parents' alcoholism dominated much of his childhood, but nobody ever mentioned it: "We could never go to a restaurant where they didn't serve beer, not even for lunch. Neither of them thought twice about driving drunk, even with us kids in the car. They'd drink every night and usually wind up in a huge fight. I remember one night they started hitting each other in an argument about whether Judy Garland or W. C. Fields was the better entertainer. My brother and I would go upstairs and try not to listen. Both of us left home at the age of seventeen. But to this day my brother refuses to believe our parents are alcoholics."

Being aware of the signs of addiction but refusing to see their significance is quite common among family members in denial about a substance abuse problem. I remember being very aware that my daughter always wore long sleeves, even in extremely hot weather, and telling myself it didn't mean anything. I noticed her boyfriend nodding off in restaurants at least twice and told myself that he must have an illness, maybe narcolepsy.

I talked to a friend who was a drug counselor and described my daughter's constant lack of money, her reluctance to spend time with me, and her extreme lethargy. "Sounds like heroin to me," my friend said.

"Oh, no. She would never do that," I said.

Just as denial allows addicts to avoid facing their substance abuse problems, it enables families to avoid confronting the problem of addiction. As long as addiction is not acknowledged, families and addicts can carry on as if nothing is wrong. Then no one experiences the anguish. It's a lot like the elephant in the living room, the one that nobody wants to talk about. Everyone knows it's there, but the whole family makes believe it isn't.

Even after families have accepted that their loved one has an addiction problem, denial is likely to persist. They may deny the depth of the problem and refuse to acknowledge all of its destructive effects. "I know she uses heroin, but she'd never shoot up," they may say. "Everyone fools around with cocaine. It's what kids do nowadays." "It's only prescription drugs. It's not like she's really an addict." "He's not a hard-core alcoholic. He only drinks beer."

By denying the seriousness of the problem, families join their loved one in the game of pretending that things "aren't that bad"—as if there were an acceptable level of addiction. It's a comforting thought that ignores the fact that addiction is a progressive disease and that it always gets worse unless it is arrested by some intervening event that opens the door to recovery.

Perhaps most damaging to families is their denial of the effects of addiction on themselves. Since addiction stunts emotional growth and keeps an addict's focus solely on self-gratification, addicts are prone to trampling all over other people's property, boundaries, and emotions. Loving family members have trouble seeing what is taking place or may minimize the addict's transgressions. They may allow themselves to be manipulated, lied to, and taken advantage of over and over again, often with the mistaken belief that they are helping the addict.

For example, Jim, a small-appliance repairman whose

brother's substance abuse problems included alcohol, crack cocaine, and amphetamines, began to notice that whenever his brother paid him a visit, a small item or sum of cash would be missing. He explained, "It would be something like a gold chain that I hadn't worn in a long time, so I'd think maybe I misplaced it. Or I'd have ten dollars less in my wallet than I thought I'd had and figured I must have spent it somewhere. One day my watch was gone, and that's when I put it all together. He'd been stealing from me for weeks, but I didn't want to see it."

Hope recalled that whenever her heroin-addicted daughter came to visit, something from the house would be missing. "I was so grateful to see her, to know she was at least alive, that I pretended not to notice," she said. "Besides, we were raising her children at that time, and I felt it was good for them to have some contact with their mother. I started leaving a twenty-dollar bill on the table so she wouldn't have to steal."

Another mother, Audrey, said that her son used to steal money from her pocketbook "all the time," but she stopped confronting him about it because he was so convincing in his denial. He also stole his father's tools and just about anything else of value he could find. "But there wasn't much that we could do about it," she said, "other than throw him out, and then his addiction might have gotten even worse."

Overlooking an addict's thefts and dishonesty is fairly common among families in the early stages of dealing with addiction. It's easier for families to ignore the problem than to confront the addict, who always has a plausible excuse at hand. When the addict says, "I'm going to the store for cigarettes" and returns three hours later, family members may pretend they have been told the truth. When the obviously impaired addict says, "I haven't used any drugs or had anything to drink," families may try to convince themselves that the addict is merely experiencing a natural low or high. I remember seeing a small drop of blood on a vein on my daughter's hand one night, an obvious puncture site, and asking her what it was. "I burned myself with a cigarette," she said offhandedly. I knew it wasn't a burn, but I tried to convince myself that she was telling the truth.

If one examines pretending and make-believe closely, the difference between unhealthy denial and healthy detachment becomes apparent. When families become detached from the addict (for more about detachment see chapter 6), they neither believe nor disbelieve what the addict says. They let go of judgment as they focus on their own well-being. On the other hand, when families engage in denial, they try to convince themselves that what they see, believe, and feel is not real. They begin to question the validity of their own perceptions. The lines between honesty and dishonesty, caring and caretaking, and reality and make-believe may blur.

"I felt I owed it to my husband to drive him to and from his counseling appointments," said one woman, "because he was at least trying to get help for his problems." She was able to overlook the fact that the counselor was easily accessible by bus and that her husband usually managed to obtain drugs during the interval between when she dropped him off and picked him up. Typically he was insensible for two or three days following his appointments.

"I knew better than to give her cash, but I bought her groceries," said one man of his heroin-addicted daughter, even when doing so left her with more money to spend on drugs.

One woman recalled waiting in her car outside a pawnshop for almost an hour while her son went in to sell some possessions. "I felt dirty sitting there, like I was doing something seedy or distasteful," she said. "But he had to sell things to pay the rent because he'd lost his job. At least that's what he told me, and I wanted to help him out."

I personally signed loans for three cars for my daughter, each of which she managed to destroy while under the influence of alcohol or other drugs. I told myself that she was a victim of bad luck, that she needed a car to get to work, and that she was trying really hard to overcome her addiction. I pretended not to notice when she came home almost unable to speak.

Denial can lead to an enormous amount of unhappiness for families as they struggle to sustain a version of reality that on some level they know is false. They suppress their suspicions, their pain, their fears, and their sense that they are somehow being "had"—that the addict is using them. Yet families may persist in their denial for a very long time because they don't know what else to do.

OBSESSED WITH THE ADDICT

In the early stages of denial, families may be able to overlook the addict's growing peculiarities, thereby avoiding the stress of facing addiction. Eventually, however, the progressive nature of the disease makes it impossible to ignore, and loving families and friends are likely to find themselves increasingly disturbed by their loved one's behavior. Even if they are still in the throes of denial, families may spend a tremendous amount of time fretting and worrying about their loved one. They may drag the addict to doctors and counselors, spend long hours discussing him or her with friends and family members, and repeatedly try to get this person to reveal "what is wrong."

I remember when I was still telling myself that my daughter's problems were no deeper than youthful confusion and possibly pot. I would often walk by the apartment house where she lived with her boyfriend, hoping for a glimpse of her so I would know she was all right. I usually didn't ring their doorbell because she had made it clear that she didn't want me interfering in her life, but I was so preoccupied with her that I was repeatedly drawn to her neighborhood. I also discussed her constantly with my other children, my closest friends, and anyone else who would listen. No matter what the initial topic of conversation, I would find some way to bring it around to my daughter. (Looking back, I'm surprised that anyone was willing to talk to me after a while!) Once, a friend pulled his car over to the side of the road because I had burst into tears and was sobbing uncontrollably for no reason that I could articulate, other than vague fears about my daughter.

Predictably, once the veil of denial was lifted and the depth of her addiction fully revealed, my preoccupation turned into full-blown obsession. She was rarely out of my mind, and my entire life became centered on her. I seemed to always have a knot of fear in my stomach. Social activities lost their appeal. I found no pleasure in anything. I cried for hours on end, and obsessive thoughts circled in my head like a gerbil on a wheel: Why had this happened? What had I done wrong? What was going to become of her? How could I make her stop?

Others experience similar responses to a loved one's addiction. The wife of a heroin addict said that she worried about her husband constantly. "He'd been clean for years when we got married, but about three years later, he confessed that he had relapsed," she said. "I started watching him like a hawk. Every time he stepped out the door, I'd feel this panic, thinking he was probably going out to score. Sometimes I'd be out driving around at eleven or twelve at night, looking for his car. I remember so many times sitting in the kitchen in the middle of the night calling every single hospital and police station I could think of to see if he'd been in an accident or OD'd. My whole world was consumed with fear for his safety and trying to make him get well."

"My mood depends on how well she's doing," observed one mother of an alcoholic. "I can gauge her state of mind within five seconds of seeing her or talking to her on the phone. If things are going okay, I can feel my mood lighten. If she's not having a good day, my spirits sink. It's like we're attached at the hip. When she cycles up, I cycle up. When she cycles down, I cycle down."

The father of a cocaine addict said of his son, "His addiction is the biggest thing in my world right now. I think about it day and night. My other kids and my wife hardly even exist anymore. There's not room for them in my head." He could have added that there was also no room for himself in his head.

As obsession deepens, family members may lose their sense of personal identity. It's as if their own lives cease to have any value, and their state of being is determined by what is going on in the addict's life rather than by what is going on in their own. They put personal goals, interests, and pleasures to the side, and their very existence only seems meaningful when it is related to the addict. If the addict is doing well, they do well; if the addict is struggling, they struggle. Even everyday experiences may be filtered through thoughts of the addict: "If only he could see this sunset, it might reawaken his appreciation of life." "If only she were here to see the baby, she might realize how much she is missing." "This is such a good movie. I know he'd get a lot out of it, if I could just convince him to see it."

As obsession with the addict blossoms, its close counterpart—compulsion—is likely to unfurl. Because the family member's peace of mind is so dependent on the addict's condition, it becomes imperative that the addict be "cured." As time goes on, "fixing" the addict becomes important not only for the addict's benefit but for the health and happiness of the well-meaning family member.

More often than not, the urge to cure the addict leads to a grim determination to take control.

THE COMPULSION TO CONTROL

The first counselor I consulted about my daughter's addiction told me, "Control is the flip side of fear." I remembered that often as my efforts to control my daughter's behavior and cure her addiction led me to behave in ways that once would have seemed unthinkable.

I had never been a particularly controlling mother. I respected my daughter's privacy, never searched her personal belongings, and more or less trusted her to make sound choices. All of that changed when I learned of her addiction. Suddenly, her business was my business. I became determined to monitor her every move.

The fear that my daughter would destroy her life or *die* was never far from my consciousness when she came home to live with me. Often, when she was asleep in the early morning, I would tiptoe downstairs and bend close to her face to make sure she was breathing. I wanted to know where she was at all times. I tried to listen in on her phone conversations; on more than one occasion, I lay on the floor with my ear pressed to a grate when she was on the phone downstairs. I searched her drawers, looked behind furniture and under her mattress, and felt along the tops of the tiles in the suspended ceiling. I went through her car early in the morning as she slept. I examined her clothing for evidence of blood spots or burn holes. I checked up on her whereabouts by calling her counselor's office or prospective employers. (Had she kept her counseling appointment? Had she gone for that job interview?) Since our voices are almost identical on the phone, I was not above calling people and pretending to be her. Once I met with a private detective to discuss the possibility of having her followed and was only deterred by a sense of shame.

I did these things in an effort to control my daughter's addiction and save her from herself. The harder I tried to save her, the more obsessed I became. My story is all too common among most families of addicts.

Eventually, the desire to control the addiction leads to the desire to control just about every aspect of the addict's life, including recovery programs, finances, housing, jobs, relationships, nutrition, exercise, health care, grooming, clothes, hobbies, attitudes, values, and even feelings. Well-intentioned family members believe that if they can get the addict properly treated and appropriately situated, the addiction will go away. They are apt to use every means at their disposal to persuade the addict to follow their plans and stop drinking or using other drugs, including the following:

Guilt	"If you loved me, you wouldn't do this."
Threats	"I'll throw you out if you don't do this."
Shame	"You're disgusting. How can you even live with yourself?"
Bribery	"I'll pay your rent for a year if you do this."
Rage	"I hate you! I don't ever want to see you again."
Tears	"You're breaking my heart."
Reasoning	"If you buy drugs instead of paying your rent, you'll become homeless."

Jack and Eileen, whose only daughter became addicted to heroin after struggling with eating disorders for many years, believed that with proper treatment their daughter would give up drugs. They sent her to some of the most highly regarded therapeutic communities in the country and paid for psychiatric treatment and residential treatment for several years.

As Jack expressed it, "Eileen and I both grew up in families where if something was wrong, you fixed it. If there was a problem, you took care of it. It was as simple as that. So when our daughter developed this problem, we said, okay. Here's how we're going to handle it. We got her into an excellent program. She completed it, and then we helped her get an apartment. She got a job, and we gave her a credit card for emergency use. We honestly believed everything was under control.

"Then we started getting these enormous credit card bills, and we finally told her we were closing the account. Then she called and told us she had relapsed, so we got her into another treatment program. To make a long story short, we spent a lot of money on different programs over three or four years. A lot of money. We were desperate. We were afraid she was going to die, and we finally had to face the fact that yes, she might die. This thing was bigger than anything we'd ever faced before. But we kept trying."

Hope and her husband took out a second mortgage on their house to pay for their daughter's first rehab treatment, because they believed she deserved "the best." When their daughter relapsed shortly after completing the program, Hope drove her daughter to state-funded treatment centers repeatedly. She said, "If she didn't like a place, she'd leave, and I'd say, 'That's okay. You deserve something better.' I'd even look over places and turn my nose up at some if I thought they weren't good enough for my daughter. I must have taken her to every detox and rehab center in the state."

Hope also found, in her mind, the ideal job for her daughter. "It was with a religious organization, and I figured being around all these church people would have a positive influence on her," Hope recalled. "She got fired for stealing five hundred dollars from them."

Audrey made it her business to call her son's counselor on a regular basis to find out how he was doing and to check up on what medications were being prescribed. "I thought the counselor and I were partners in this since we both wanted my son to get clean. We could kind of work together, you know? At first he was polite, but after a while, he told me I should get my own counselor and stay out of my son's business. He finally stopped taking my calls," Audrey said, cringing at the memory. That didn't stop her from trying another approach. "I got so worried about my son I started calling the police and telling them when he was going out. 'He's gonna have drugs on him,' I'd say. I thought if he went to jail, he'd get clean. They'd tell me there wasn't much they could do about it."

Andy, married less than a year when his wife developed an addiction to painkillers, decided that the best way to solve the problem was to put her on a strict budget. He said, "I made her give me her paycheck every week. I gave her twenty-five dollars for lunch and spending money on Mondays, and it had to last. I put the credit cards and checking account in my name only. I followed her to the gas station and paid for her gas. I bought the groceries. I didn't see how she could possibly afford to keep buying pills. But she managed. I think she was shoplifting, although she never admitted it."

Deb promised her addicted boyfriend that she'd marry him only after he'd been clean for at least a year. She settled for six months. Her hope that his heroin addiction was cured soon gave way to despair as he resumed his old pattern of sobriety and relapse. "It's like having your very own five-year-old child," she said, "and you have to watch out for him or something may happen, like the house may burn down or he may get into a car accident."

Celeste thought that reasoning would be the best way to persuade her son to get the help he needed for his addiction. "We'd have these long conversations about what addiction was doing to his life," she recalled, "and I'd feel like I'd really gotten through to him. I'd explain how addicts can't do it alone; they need to be in some kind of program to get better. I'd point out how drugs were ruining his life and how he had all these good qualities that were just being destroyed. He'd agree and seemed sincere. But after I left he probably went and shot up again. I don't know. We had these conversations over and over, and his problems just got worse and worse."

In their efforts to control the addict, many families become amateur detectives. They listen in on phone conversations and check out every unfamiliar number on their phone bill. They open the addict's mail and pore over bills and financial statements. They check the mileage on the addict's car, examine the addict's clothing, count prescriptions, go through the addict's personal belongings with a fine-tooth comb, and engage in cat-and-mouse conversations aimed at uncovering some recent falsehood. "So. What time did you leave work today?" they might ask when they know the addict took three hours to make the half-hour trip home. "How was the AA meeting?" they may inquire when they know that the addict did not attend the meeting.

Others prefer a more direct assault. "Where are you going and what time will you be back?" they ask. "Where have you been?" "Why are your eyes so red?" "Why are you wearing long sleeves?" "You look tired. What have you been doing?"

Whatever methods families choose to try to control the addict—and most of us try them all at one time or another—their efforts rarely produce the positive results they so desperately seek. What's more, by focusing so intently on their addicted loved one, their own emotional, and often physical, health is likely to be compromised.

SICKENED BY ADDICTION

Sick at heart is the way most of us feel when faced with the addiction of someone we love. The phrase captures the suffering that family members endure and hints at addiction's subtle, pernicious effects on the overall health of everyone concerned.

Families undergo enormous prolonged stress when they confront a loved one's addiction. They experience near-constant worry about immediate concerns: "Will the rent be paid?" "Has he let the car insurance lapse?" "Is she going to lose this job too?" Crushing fears about the future abound as well: "Is she going to turn to prostitution?" "Is he going to end up on the streets?" "Are they going to send her to jail?" "Is he going to die?" On top of their worry and fear, families experience the confusion that comes from repeatedly being lied to, the anxiety of never knowing what the next crisis will be, the frustration of doing everything within their power to help someone who refuses to be helped, the sorrow of watching a loved one slip away, and the disappointment of having their hopes raised only to be dashed yet another time.

It's no wonder that so many families of addicts suffer at least some of the ill-effects of stress, which can include headaches, backaches, bowel problems, ulcers, high blood pressure, and heart disease, as well as insomnia, fatigue, appetite disorders, loss of sexual desire, exhaustion, and depression.

"I was out of my mind," Celeste recalled. "I couldn't sleep,

and I was exhausted all the time. I'd go to the store for ba-
nanas and come home with broccoli. I'd be driving down a
road and forget where I was going. I'd take an order from a
customer and forget what they said before I hung up the
phone. People must have thought I was nuts."

Other family members say such things as "I didn't go out
for two years after I found out about my daughter's addiction." "I started taking antidepressants because all I did was
cry." "Every day I'd go through the motions, you know, go to
work, act like everything was all right, go home. But he was
always there in my head." "I forgot how to have fun." "I
walked around feeling like I'd been kicked in the gut. I never
smiled."

Dealing with addiction can drain all the joy out of life,
leading concerned family members to exist in a perpetual
state of anxious exhaustion. The collateral damage of addiction doesn't stop there. Marriages can become strained as parents disagree about the best course of action. Children and
spouses can feel abandoned as a family member showers un-
wavering attention on the addict and neglects everyone else.

"It seems like you have to be an alcoholic to get any attention in this family," a sibling may complain. "I don't have a
wife anymore. All she thinks about is our son," a husband may
say. Siblings or others close to the situation may see (with
perfect clarity) that the addict is being rewarded for bad behavior when the family pays the car insurance bill or gives the
addict yet another "loan" or finds the addict yet another job,
apartment, counselor, or lawyer.

Under such unhappy circumstances, resentment and
anger can build. One woman recalled that one of her other
sons beat up the addicted son on more than one occasion,
trying to knock some sense in him. One father routinely be-
rated his middle-aged alcoholic son with such comments as

"You're a bum! You're disgusting. Look at what you've become. You're scum!"

Even those who have been the most patient with the addict, the most forgiving and loving and uncomplaining, may sometimes find themselves filled with rage. It is hardly surprising. Healthy love can flourish only within an environment of mutual respect and consideration, qualities that are in short supply in most addicts. Instead, addicts repeatedly hurt and disappoint the very people who care the most about them, and anger is a natural result.

One mother confessed that she was shocked to find herself screeching angrily at her heroin-addicted son one day. "I stopped by his house to see how he was doing, and for some reason I just snapped," she said. "The place was a pigsty, and he looked like a zombie. I lost it. I said, 'You're not even human anymore. You don't have any feelings, no emotions. You don't take pleasure in anything that's real. You don't care if the sun comes up or if it never comes up. You're nothing but a parasite, a hollow-eyed junkie. You disgust me!'"

One father admitted that he sometimes fantasized about hiring someone to beat some sense into his alcoholic son.

Some family members admit to harboring a secret wish that the addict would die. "At least I could mourn him and get on with my life," they may reason. "She's not really living anyway. God might as well take her so I can stop worrying," they may say. "Don't I deserve a little peace of mind before I die?"

Such sentiments are indicative of the deep suffering that many families of addicts experience. A sense of hopelessness arises when every conceivable effort to save the addict has failed. When families have given everything they have to give, and when the only result seems to be endless unhappiness, they may long for an escape no matter what the cost.

What such families tend to forget is that they do not have

to wait until their addict has found recovery before they can begin to enjoy life again. In fact, families can begin to rediscover simple pleasures and to feel happiness and peace of mind. They can even begin to laugh again—*no matter what the addict is doing.* (I was shocked when I first heard this idea. It took months before I could begin to believe it.)

The key is for families to begin their own journey of recovery. The journey includes learning healthier ways of interacting with their addicted loved one and embarking on a path of self-healing. As long as addicts and family members are locked in the destructive cycle of addiction, there is actually little hope that things will get better. "If nothing changes, nothing changes," as they say in Twelve Step meetings.

Family members who choose to break the unhealthy cycle can have a positive influence on their addicted loved one and reaffirm the value of their own lives.

FIVE

THE PROCESS OF CHANGE

A friend of mine has been trying to quit smoking for years. She's tried everything she could think of: patches, gum, hypnosis, support groups, and therapy. She even taped some lurid pictures of smokers' lungs around her house, convinced that the glaring ugliness of the images would deter her from smoking. But her smoke-free lifestyle has never taken hold, and in a matter of weeks or months (once it was almost two years), she finds herself lighting up again. "I've seen the literature. I know the statistics," she'll say. "I'm killing myself, and at the very least I feel like a social pariah, hunching in doorways during my breaks at work. What will it take to make me stop?"

What indeed? My friend is facing the challenge of making a personal change, a challenge that substance abusers and their families know all too well. If changing our habits, attitudes, or desires were simply a matter of identifying a problem and deciding to fix it, then there would be little need for the self-help movement, psychoanalysis, or addiction treatment programs—or books like this! But the reality is that making any significant personal change is an often daunting task. Add to that the psychological and physiological power of psychoactive substances, and the enormity of overcoming addiction becomes apparent.

It is, perhaps, the sheer magnitude of the challenges faced by addicts and their families that has led us to think of addiction treatment in terms of "recovery" rather than simply "change." Change connotes altering certain habits, perhaps replacing one pattern of behavior with another. On the other hand, recovery suggests something deeper and more profound—an inner transformation that broadens an individual's psychological and spiritual sensibilities.

A speaker I heard at an AA meeting alluded to this fundamental difference when he told the audience, "The man I was will always drink." He had become a new person, he suggested, with a new outlook on life and a different understanding of his world, and it was this personal revolution that enabled him to remain sober. When those in the addiction community speak of "white-knuckling it" or a "dry drunk," they are referring to individuals who have stopped drinking or taking drugs but who have not achieved the self-awareness and personal growth that comes with recovery in its fullest sense. Certainly it is possible for some individuals to become abstinent without achieving recovery, and abstinence is in itself a monumental victory. But for many, the process of overcoming addiction requires the willingness to embrace a significant change in attitudes and perceptions.

Individuals who are "in recovery" are not just the same people with different habits. They are people who have experienced an inner enlightenment, people whose new choices and behaviors spring naturally from a transformed inner self. It's a lofty concept that has its roots in myths and religious teachings that speak to the power of human beings to re-invent themselves and begin anew.

"This is all well and good," you may be thinking, "but it's the addict who needs recovery, not the family. After all, it's the addict who has the problem." This is superficially true, but as we saw in the previous chapter, many families eventually join their addicted loved one in a maze of denial, obsession, and unhealthy behaviors. And although there are vast differences between an addict's and a family's search for recovery, there are distinct similarities.

For addicts, recovery implies a healing process that includes stopping the use of alcohol or other drugs, replacing harmful habits with healthful habits, and discovering some larger purpose that adds meaning to their lives. For families, recovery usually means healing the obsessive-compulsive relationship with the addict, replacing negative behaviors with positive ones, gleaning some lasting wisdom, and enhancing the quality of their own lives and, perhaps, the life of their addicted loved one.

Fortunately, even if the addict is not ready to embrace recovery, families can begin their own journey at any time. In fact, when the family begins to get well, interpersonal dynamics change, often sparking the desire for recovery in the addict. To see how the process works, consider the following fundamental principles of how people change.

THE PROCESS OF CHANGE

Most of us make large or small changes regularly throughout our lives. We get married or divorced, buy a new house, go back to school, find a different job, change our hair color, cancel a magazine subscription, take up a new hobby, go on a diet, redecorate the living room, and so on. Change is so natural, so inevitable, that we seldom stop to think about the process. However, sociologists and psychologists have given the matter some attention and have constructed a general blueprint of how people change.

The best-known model of change was proposed by James

Prochaska, Ph.D., and his co-authors in *Changing for Good*. Prochaska became interested in how people break bad habits partly because of his own father's struggle with alcoholism. According to Prochaska, regardless of whether people are attempting to make large or small changes, they all go through the same six stages of change.

The first stage is called *precontemplation*. This stage is characterized by lack of awareness. Some people in this stage may have an inkling that there's a problem, but they are not even considering doing something about it. Others have no idea that there's anything wrong. Even when problems are causing difficulties in their lives, people in this stage are resistant to the concept of change. Precontemplation can be summed up by the words of eighteenth-century social commentator G. K. Chesterson: "It isn't that they can't see the solution, it's that they can't see the problem."

The second stage is *contemplation*. This stage is one of growing awareness. Individuals begin to see that there are problems or that certain changes would be beneficial. Sometimes, but not always, a confrontation or a crisis brings about this growing awareness, such as when your doctor tells you to lose weight or your mate walks out on you. Those in this stage are beginning to think about their problems but are not yet ready to do anything about them.

The third stage is *preparation*. People rarely make immediate changes. Rather, they take their time thinking about the problems and evaluating their options. During the preparation stage of change, individuals start making inquiries, consider possible courses of action, and decide what steps they will take to make a change.

The fourth stage is *action*. In this stage, individuals are taking steps to alter their behavior. Whether small and tentative or large and bold, the actions taken during this stage are intended to move individuals closer to the successful resolution of their problems. For example, people in this stage may have enrolled in a class, bought an exercise cycle, entered rehab, or made an appointment with a credit counselor. The key is that they have engaged in some tangible act to address their problems and effect change.

The fifth stage is *maintenance*. This stage gets to the crux of the matter. Almost anyone can give up chocolate or begin an exercise program or turn off the television—once! It's the *permanent* establishment of a new pattern, a new habit, a new way of looking at things that's hard to accomplish. Ask anyone who's ever broken a New Year's resolution, which probably includes anyone who's ever made one. Because this stage is almost always the most difficult, relapses to earlier stages—even to the precontemplation stage—are common. That's okay. In Prochaska's view, progress is seldom linear. That is, people rarely set out on a course of change and proceed directly to their goal. Rather, they experience change as a spiral, where they inch forward, then backward. Move up, then down. The good news is that even as they relapse to earlier stages, they absorb lessons learned along the way. They are not completely unchanged, even though those changes may not be visible to others—or to themselves.

The sixth and final stage is *termination*. This stage is reached when the problem no longer exists, when the temptation to relapse is no longer present. Some psychologists doubt that this stage is ever fully experienced, noting, for example, that smokers who have been clean for twenty-five years or more may experience an occasional craving, even relapse. Nevertheless, those who have reached this stage have successfully incorporated change into their lives, making new habits, thoughts, or attitudes (often all three) integral parts of who they are.

The value of the stages of change model is that it helps us to recognize that change is a process with a predictable pattern and that setbacks are an almost inevitable part of the process. It is unreasonable to expect that everything can get better all at once or to fear that one mistake or relapse will negate the progress that's been made. Setbacks come with the territory, and some people must move through the spiral of change many times before they are able to achieve and maintain their goals.

Although Prochaska's model proposes a useful blueprint for understanding the general process of change, the larger questions, perhaps, are the following: Why is it that some people can go merrily along in the same damaging or dead-end routine for months and even years before they begin to realize that they need to do something about their lives? And why is it that even when they recognize that something is harming them, they are still frozen in inaction for a long time before taking those first tentative steps toward change?

More to the point, what does it take for an addict to decide to change?

THE ADDICT'S ROAD TO RECOVERY

A twenty-two-year-old woman who had been addicted to heroin since the age of sixteen was living a life of utter destitution. After serving a six-month jail sentence, she began spending her nights in a "wet shelter" (a shelter that does not require its clients to be clean and sober), sharing quarters with street people of all ages and an army of cockroaches. Turned out of the shelter at seven each morning, she spent her days shoplifting or turning tricks, getting drugs and getting high, and huddling in the public library for warmth. She had attended dozens of treatment facilities over the years and spent hundreds of hours with counselors. Nothing worked, and she seemed destined to be destroyed by addiction. However, one day everything changed.

"I remember lying in the shelter one morning, shivering and shivering because I was dope sick," she recalled. "One of the women who worked there asked if I wanted to go to a detox, and I said yes. I knew they'd give me something for the pain. She punched out and used her own time to drive me to a detox center, which was really nice of her. They were busy that day, and I had to sit in the waiting room for eight hours. I watched *Titanic* twice on their little TV. While I was sitting there, this thought came to me: 'All I have to do not to live like this anymore is stop using drugs.' It was so simple— but so powerful. For years people had been telling me basically the same thing. Yet I never got it before. But that moment was the start of my recovery. I haven't used a drug since, and I've been clean for three years."

Why this particular moment for this particular young woman? There is no way to definitively answer that question. Perhaps lessons learned during repeated journeys through the spiral of change finally came together for her. Perhaps she was at a stage of psychological readiness. Perhaps she had finally reached her "bottom."

The mystery of why people start to get better at any given moment will probably always remain just that, a mystery. Yet certain factors seem to contribute to the desire to change no matter how long the process may take. One factor is the accumulation of knowledge. Each time an individual enters a higher stage in the process of change (going from contemplation to preparation, for example), understanding of the problem may expand, and self-awareness may grow. Even mistakes and relapses can lead to greater knowledge that may one day translate into the awareness and motivation necessary to make sustainable changes.

Jane, a heroin addict who was on the streets and in and

out of jail over an eight-year period, described her recovery experiences this way: "Little things happened to me over the years. I remember looking through the prison fence, watching cars go by, and saying to this woman, 'Ooh, look at that one. Look at that one! When I get out, I'm going to ride in a car like that, 'cause I love cars.' And she gave me a look with those dead eyes of hers—she was in for life and everyone who's doing life has dead eyes—and said, 'The only difference between you and me is you get to go out for a while and ride in those cars, but you always come back.' And I thought, 'She's right.'

"Another time I was in jail over Christmastime, and I called my mother. I think she knew I was there, but she didn't write to me. And I asked if she would please send me pictures of my kids, and she did. I was so happy. And actually I started going to church when I was in prison, and every time I went to church I would bawl my eyes out. So I told these people my mother sent me pictures of my kids, and I got classified for prerelease. The church people said, 'See, God's working in your life.'

"When I got out, I went into a sober house. I had to go to meetings and I would listen to people's stories, but inside nothing changed. I thought to myself, 'If I have to stay sober and go to these damn meetings, then I'm going to steal stuff and I'm going to look good.' I got a sponsor. I got my one month, two months, three months clean. At five months I don't know what happened, but I wanted to get high. I was crawling out of my skin. I couldn't stand it and had to get high. I was so mad that I couldn't just go out and buy a bag of heroin because you gotta buy works [syringe, cooker, and so on], find out where to buy it. So I put these cans of Spam together, and I tried to inhale it. I used to inhale all kinds of stuff when I was a kid: deodorant, furniture polish, everything. So I'm trying to inhale this Spam, and I thought, 'What the hell am I doing?' I put it down. I think that's where my recovery started."

However, Jane returned to drugs and then to prison one last time before her recovery finally took hold. She recalled: "When I got out of prison, they sent me to this halfway house that was brand new. Some AA women had started it. I was the only resident, and they didn't even have a director yet. So they'd come over and talk to me and take me shopping because all I had was my prison clothes. When I finished my six months, the newspaper did a story about me, and all these politicians were there for the photographs. And the women asked me to stay on as house manager, and it just grew from there. I think I didn't want to let them down."

For Jane, the accumulation of experiences, many of them terrible, some of them glimmers of light, slowly built the foundation for recovery. Seven years later, Jane is still clean. She went back to school, bought a house, and works as a counselor for addicted women.

Another factor in the decision to change is the accumulation of suffering. One night, not long after my daughter came home to live with me, I remember calling a crisis hot line to ask what I could do to help my daughter get off drugs. "She's so miserable. I know she wants to stop," I said, fighting back tears.

The man on the other end, a recovering addict, was not impressed. "A lot of people want a lot of things," he said. "I want a million bucks. But am I willing to do what it takes to get it? No." He went on to explain that *wanting* recovery— that is, wishing that it would somehow magically happen— and making a commitment to *getting* recovery no matter what the cost are two very different things. And until my daughter reached that level of commitment, she would probably not get better.

"What will it take to get her there?" I asked.

His answer frightened me.

"A lot of pain."

She had already suffered a lot of pain—the loss of her high school sweetheart, the loss of all her possessions, jobs, apartments, friends, opportunities, and self-respect—but perhaps all that was not enough. Perhaps the rewards, the *pleasure* that the drugs delivered, outweighed the suffering she endured.

"An addict has to hit bottom before he wants to recover," the man on the phone continued. "And no one knows what his bottom is until he gets there."

The concept of hitting bottom is often used in the recovery community. It implies a situation so unbearable that getting better becomes the only viable option. When we think of "bottoms," we envision homelessness, jail, and dire physical illness. But not all addicts reach such depths before seeking and finding recovery. As one therapist expressed it, "You can get off the elevator at any floor." Most therapists agree that a primary goal for those who are trying to help an addict should be to "raise the bottom," that is, to nudge the addict toward recovery before the addict's life is in total ruin.

Mark, a married alcoholic with two children, recalled his "bottom" this way: "I'd been drinking heavily for years, and it was doing terrible things to my wife and kids. They couldn't stand being around me. I'd walk into a room, and they'd leave. I was an embarrassment. I looked like hell. I stank. On the job I was messing up all the time, but the boss was a friend and he kept letting me slide. I started getting really sick, and finally my wife made a doctor's appointment for me. She could barely stand me by then, but she's a compassionate person. She knew I was suffering. The doctor told me I didn't have long to live if I kept drinking. That was it. Stop drinking or die young. I started going to AA, and I haven't had a drink since."

He added, "Everyone's bottom is different. I never lost my family, my home, or my job. I was lucky. Given the choice of life or death, I chose life."

Not everyone can identify his or her decision to get clean so precisely. Not everyone finds recovery at the same pace or in the same way. But addicts who make the transition from being an active user to a recovering addict seem to follow similar steps along their journeys. These steps include becoming aware of the problems addiction is causing in their lives, experiencing deep unhappiness with their situations, deciding that they want to overcome their addictions, and finding meaningful support for their efforts to recover.

As one therapist who has worked with addicted clients for more than twenty-five years explained, "Most addicts want to get clean, even if they are not ready to admit it. I don't know anyone who likes waking up dope sick every day. I don't know anyone who says, 'When I was a kid my goal was to sell my body on the street or to live in crack houses and go to jail.' They have a terrible disease, but most of them want to get better. The trick is to tap into that desire and help them build on it."

He went on to say that three things affect how somebody changes: (1) the unique set of strengths, weaknesses, and resources, including personality and family, the individual brings to the situation; (2) the skills and tools, including education and awareness, the individual acquires through treatment and experience; and (3) the support of a healing relationship with somebody else, such as a therapist, minister, or sponsor (a mentor in a Twelve Step program such as Alcoholics Anonymous or Narcotics Anonymous), who can help the individual mobilize personal strengths on his or her own.

The recovery experiences of Lia, a twenty-two-year-old addict and alcoholic who has been clean and sober for more than a year, illustrate the complex and often lengthy process of overcoming addiction: "When I was seventeen, my parents put me into rehab. When I came out, I knew I wasn't going to give up drinking. I wasn't going to give up drugs. I still wanted to use heroin once in a while. I still thought I could do it.

"I got arrested for selling acid and spent three months in jail, and all I could think about was when I get out, I'm going to get a real job, go to school, go to the gym. Yet the first thing I did when I got out was use. I didn't want to live that lifestyle, but the other part of me couldn't wait to get out and shoot heroin.

"I wanted a good life, but I wanted to be able to get high. That was my goal, to be able to control my use of substances so I could be happy and still use. That was my goal since I was thirteen, trying to find a substance I could do and still be able to maintain life—still be able to drink and have fun, still be able to get high on heroin, but not have consequences.

"I had a month left on my probation that I wanted to clear up, so my parole officer advised me to go into rehab. I was living in a shelter because my parents wouldn't let me live with them, and I was still shooting up. I hated myself for using. I wanted to get clean, but I thought I had to do it myself. No one could help me. I'm unique. I'm different. And I never thought I'd give up drinking.

"So I got into a rehab, planning to stay just a month. I wanted to get clean really, really bad, but I didn't think recovery [Twelve Step programs] was how I was going to do it. I thought there were choices: I could go into recovery, I could move, or I could change my life this way or that. I thought there were options. Now I know recovery was my only option. Now I know there was no way in hell I could've ever gotten clean if I hadn't gotten into recovery. And most people out there who are using can't get clean and sober [without recovery], and if they do, they're miserable.

"Anyway, in rehab they talked about a Higher Power. I didn't know what that meant. I mean, I love nature and sunsets—things I obviously didn't make. Something bigger than me made them. I didn't see what that had to do with my life. But someone suggested I pray. That night and the next morning I got on my knees. I don't even know what I said. I just jumped up and started laughing, like 'Whoa. I can't believe I just did that.' I did that a few times. I didn't know if I believed in God. I felt ridiculous.

"I remember when I was sitting in group one day having a craving, and I could see myself sitting on the toilet or sitting on the bathroom floor, 'cause that's where I used to get high a lot. Instead of seeing the high, I saw the empty house and myself feeling like shit after the ringer. And that's what I remembered. I thought, 'Oh my God, this worked; maybe there is a power bigger than myself.' This thing is so much bigger than me. I can't control it. I thought for so long I had willpower and could stop. Now I realize that whatever made me out there is higher than me. That's the only thing that can help me.

"I stayed in rehab the whole six months and went to meetings [Narcotics Anonymous or Alcoholics Anonymous] every day for a year. Now I work Monday through Friday from nine to six. I go to meetings four nights a week and twice on Sundays. I go out and speak at meetings on Thursdays. I go to college one night a week. I hang out with my friends on Saturdays. That's my day off. I go to concerts, and you know what? I found out I can have fun without drinking. I used to always dance with a drink in my hand.

"But I don't take anything for granted. I know I'll always have this disease, just like some people have cancer or an allergy to something. I have an allergy to substances. I just hope I'm still clean a year from now. I will be."

Although Lia's early treatment experiences were not immediately successful, it is likely that some of the knowledge she gained stayed with her. By the time she was psychologically ready to get better (although she still resisted the idea of recovery and total abstinence), she was fortunate to enter a rehabilitation center that provided the support she needed. There she experienced an inner transformation—in her case, she found a Higher Power—that sustained her through difficult moments. She continues to get support from her sponsor and other recovering addicts in her Twelve Step meetings.

OBSTACLES TO RECOVERY

Anyone looking at the hardships that Lia (like most addicts) endured during her years of active addiction might be puzzled by the inner conflict she felt over giving up substances. After all, alcohol and other drugs had brought her to her knees. Wouldn't she welcome the opportunity to rid herself of them forever? Wouldn't she regard them as an enemy rather than a temptation?

In fact, most addicts experience deep conflict about giving up their drugs of choice. As we have seen, change is hard for everyone. In addition, substances of abuse actually alter brain function, diminishing the ability to make rational decisions. And addiction creates physical and psychological dependence that can't easily be overcome.

But the ambivalence over whether or not to fight addiction goes deeper than that. Giving up alcohol or other drugs has far-reaching implications for addicts. After all, no matter how much misery the addiction has created, it has also provided significant rewards: the pleasure of feeling high, the sense of kinship with others who are making the same choices, the release from pain and stress, and the escape from overwhelming difficulties. Fighting addiction means becoming willing to face problems, perhaps for the first time, without a chemical crutch.

It means becoming willing to accept consequences of past mistakes and to assume adult responsibilities. It often means giving up certain acquaintances, a lifestyle, and a sense of identity. It means saying good-bye forever to familiar behaviors and replacing them with new and often awkward-feeling choices. It usually means enduring suffering, anxiety, and depression without the numbing effects of substances.

Because of these many obstacles, for many addicts, the fear of getting clean is greater than their fear of destitution and death. Yet sooner or later, most addicts do make some attempt to overcome their addiction. When they do, they face serious obstacles. Foremost among these is the power of the drugs themselves.

A body that is accustomed to the presence of an addictive substance screams out for that substance when it is withheld. These cravings are both psychological and physiological in nature and, according to most addicts, they are unimaginably powerful.

In Lia's words, "Early recovery is the worst place to be. You're crazy. I didn't know if I was coming or going. One minute I'd think, 'I'm really going to do this,' and then I'd just want to get out of there [rehab]. I'd get a craving really bad, a head rush, like an electric shock through your whole body, and I'd really want it. I'd just really want to get high. I'd be sitting there, and all of a sudden I'd just want it so bad. I still do now."

Another obstacle to recovery is the addict's own despair. Often addicts feel a great deal of shame about themselves, remorse for the harm they have caused others, and hopelessness about their ability to fix past mistakes. I remember confronting my daughter when I discovered evidence of her using and making some scathing remark about how great she must feel. Crying, she said, "It doesn't make me feel good. I feel so weak when I do it. I hate myself."

An alcoholic said, "When I saw the look in my kids' eyes and saw what I was doing to them, I felt like a piece of shit. I drank to pass out."

A cocaine addict recalled, "When I thought about getting clean, I'd feel sick. I'd lost my house, my car, my job, my driver's license. I had a ton of bills. Everybody was after me. I couldn't face it."

Jane, who lost custody of her two children during her years of addiction, said, "When I was in prison, these girls would say, 'I'm never going to do drugs again. I'm never coming back here.' And I said, 'When I get out, I'm doing a bag of dope.' That's what I lived for, because I'd already given my kids up and I accepted it. I couldn't fix the problem. How could I take these two small children back and tell them I was so sorry?"

As if confronting cravings, self-loathing, and enormous problems weren't enough, many addicts seeking recovery also struggle with some form of mental or emotional illness. As we saw in chapter 3, a significant number of addicts have underlying emotional or psychiatric conditions. Individuals who are suffering from co-occurring disorders—including schizophrenia, bipolar disorder, anxiety, and clinical depression— face major hurdles when fighting addiction. For these individuals, substance abuse has become the only path to feeling "normal"—to escaping the fear, confusion, emptiness, boredom, and pain within. I will never forget the words of my own daughter, who had suffered from depression since early adolescence, as I drove her to her first detox. She huddled in the seat beside me, looked straight ahead, and said in a small, bleak voice, "I feel so empty inside." What would fill that gaping hole within if not drugs?

Finally, addicts who want to get clean may face the obstacle of not having the tools and support they need to succeed. As with any problem, the more you know about it, the better your chances are of solving it. Too many addicts try to fight addiction with willpower, with "geographical cures" (going someplace new), by switching substances, or by employing other techniques that are almost always doomed to failure. When they fail, addicts feel worse about themselves and return to their best (and in some cases their only) friend: their drug of choice. Addicts need to understand the effects of substances on their minds and bodies to learn how to combat the pernicious nature of their disease and to know that somebody is there to offer support and encouragement over the long struggle ahead.

Although families cannot solve their loved one's substance abuse problems (addicts must accept full responsibility for their own recovery), they can often play a meaningful role in the addict's search for recovery. In the next chapter we will see how families can promote their loved one's recovery and explore some helpful ways for families themselves to recover from the damaging impact of addiction.

SIX

PATHS TO RECOVERY

A cliché in the treatment community is "Insanity is doing the same things over and over and expecting different results." The truth of this phrase is most evident when dealing with an addicted loved one. In our desperation to bring about some positive change, most of us try the same things again and again—from nagging and scolding, to threatening and pleading, to fixing and problem-solving—only to be devastated anew with each relapse or rebuff from the addict.

To make matters worse, many families come to believe that they themselves can never be happy until their loved one "straightens up." They put their own lives on hold and in a sense become hostage to the addiction, abdicating responsibility for their own well-being. As their loved one's compulsion to drink or use other drugs continues, their own compulsion to change and control the addict intensifies. Thus the addict and the family become locked in a maze in which well-worn paths lead only to stress and unhappiness, never release.

Trying to help someone overcome addiction can be like walking through a minefield. At each step our best efforts can blow up in front of us, often seeming to make the addiction worse. Trying to change somebody else is always a risky business. It is human nature to resist others' attempts to force us to change. We want to be responsible for our own choices and lives no matter how much of a mess we might be making of things. When other people tell us we need to change, they seem to be telling us we are wrong. This is criticism, and it cuts deepest when we fear it is true.

The other reason our efforts to help an addict can seem so futile is that the power of human persuasion is no match for the overwhelming power of addiction. Imagine trying to force someone to give up smoking or lose weight. It is simply not possible to exercise our will over another person's psyche. The resolve to give up smoking, fatty foods, overspending, or any number of detrimental, compulsive behaviors that we humans engage in, including alcohol or other drug abuse, can only come from the person who is engaging in those behaviors. Nothing allows us to get inside somebody else's brain and engineer the change in feelings, attitudes, and perceptions that form the foundation of any successful recovery.

That said, families can be of enormous value in helping their addicted loved one to reach a state of readiness for recovery, in "raising the bottom" for their loved one, and in supporting their loved one through the recovery process. They can do this by becoming healthier themselves and by employing some simple, effective strategies for dealing with addiction. Keep in mind that there is no "cookie-cutter" approach that will "solve" the problem of addiction, no "one-size-fits-all" solution to this deviously complex disease. Instead, there are general principles that can help families sow seeds of recovery for both their loved one and, most important, for themselves. By choosing to seek recovery, families can begin to reaffirm the value of their own lives and—perhaps—light the way for their addicted loved one.

PROMOTING THE ADDICT'S RECOVERY

Remember, no one can get another person clean and sober. The impetus for that change and the will to carry it out must come from somewhere within the very core of the addicted individual. However, external influences—including interactions with family members—can affect the progression of the disease of addiction. Although families do not have the power to cure the disease, they do have the power to create a recovery-oriented base of support for their loved one. The following strategies can help them do just that.

Get Educated

When my daughter was a sophomore in high school, her behavior changed in disturbing ways. She dropped out of activities that she used to enjoy, including dance and voice lessons; she began skipping classes and was chronically late for school; her grades plummeted; she began selling personal possessions; her personal habits became slovenly; and she began lying to me on a habitual basis.

I suspected depression and took her to at least four child psychologists during the next two years. She refused to open up to any of them, but they all told me more or less the same thing: that my daughter was a normal teenager with a good head on her shoulders who was going through a particularly rough version of typical teen rebellion. I had nothing to worry about. Time would solve the problem.

None of them suggested that she might have a drug problem, and I was too deeply into my own denial to even consider the possibility. It was only years later, after she had cycled down into heroin addiction, that she revealed that she had taken more than fifty LSD trips in high school and had been habitually stoned on pot. In retrospect, I can now see that most of her disturbing behaviors were classic symptoms of substance abuse.

I tell this story not to chastise the counseling profession—although I do feel that those four psychologists failed me and my daughter—but to illustrate the point that despite the enormous amounts of money being spent on the nation's war on drugs, there remains a dangerous lack of knowledge about drugs and their effects, not just among families, but among mental health professionals as well. It seems to me that if we put fewer resources into harsh and ineffective punitive measures and devoted more resources to education, we would be more successful in our battle against addiction. Knowledge, in the long run, is our most effective weapon against this terrible disease.

Addiction is truly one of the great social and medical dilemmas of our time. When addiction enters a family system, familiar relationships, rules, and routines are shaken. Certain rock-solid beliefs may fly out the window. During the early, shocking days of acknowledging the addiction, most families flounder through an emotional quagmire. Eventually, they seek answers. This is an important first step. Getting educated about addiction is essential if families are to have any realistic hope of helping their loved one. In this respect, addiction is no different than any other disease: the more you understand about its nature, effects, and treatment, the better your chances are of combating the disease. A list of helpful sources of information, including books and Web sites, appears at the back of this book. You can also ask questions of professionals, especially counselors specializing in substance abuse.

Don't forget Twelve Step meetings. Taking part in an Al-Anon group, which focuses on helping families of addicts, may be critical for maintaining your own sense of well-being while learning about the disease. Try to get an Al-Anon sponsor who is available for telephone calls and meetings. Attending a few open Alcoholics Anonymous or Narcotics Anonymous meetings is an excellent way to deepen your understanding of your loved one's situation. People who speak at these meetings are almost always in recovery, and their stories are usually enlightening and inspiring. The bottom line is this: the more families know about addiction, the better chance they have of helping their loved one.

Be Supportive

Being supportive does not mean we allow others to take advantage of us. It does mean showing others that we care, offering encouragement, and treating them with respect. Being supportive also implies that we ourselves are healthy and stable enough to provide support to others.

Addicts need to know that others care about them and believe they will get well. It is important that they hear such words as "I love you," "you're making good progress," and "I'm here to help." Even if such remarks appear to make absolutely no difference, most addicts, like most people, will store these positive messages for later use. A friend of mine recalled that years ago, when she was falling apart over a broken relationship, a friend said, "I know you'll get through this because you're so grounded." She told me, "Ever since then, anytime I've felt totally lost, I remember that I'll get through it because I'm a grounded person."

Jane recalled that during her years of active addiction, she often remembered the words of a favorite uncle who had reassured her mother, "Don't worry about Jane. Jane's going to be all right." She said, "I lived on that. I still do."

As one therapist explained, "Caustic words are rejected. They bounce off the person. Words like 'I love you,' 'I care,'

'I believe in you' are stickier. In a sense, they stick to the addict's skin and later work their way inside when they can have a positive effect."

But before they learn to listen to these words of encouragement, addicts usually end up alienating a lot of people. Being supportive is difficult when what you're feeling frustrated, angry, or outraged. Sometimes families may have to distance themselves from their loved one in order to preserve their own dignity or peace of mind, which in the end will enable them to encourage and support others. In a sense, families must first move away from the addict to move closer.

Sometimes an addict's behavior can become so destructive that the family chooses to limit contact with the addict or to ask the addict to move out of the family home. In these situations, families can still be supportive by expressing themselves in terms of wanting to help. They can say to someone whose addiction is creating havoc in the home, "You can't live with us right now because being here isn't helping you. We can't give you what you need." They can then suggest alternative living arrangements such as a residential program. This is especially important in the case of minor children.

The decision to ask a minor child to leave home is one that should be made only with professional guidance and only as a last resort. One counselor observed, "Parents who are advised to use 'tough love' sometimes think the best answer is to throw the kid out. These kids often end up getting into things they may never have gotten into if their parents had taken a different approach."

Even when families make the painful decision to distance themselves from their loved one, they can frame their decision in terms of care and support: "We love you. We believe in you. When you're ready to get help, we'll be here for you."

Let Crises Happen

One of my favorite sayings from Al-Anon literature is "In nature there are no punishments or rewards. There are consequences." This statement takes the right or wrong out of a situation, removes labels, and offers the plain, objective observation that choices have consequences. In scientific jargon, for every action there is a reaction. This is an important lesson for addicts to learn. They must learn it if they are to begin recovery.

The human psychological maturation process requires the ability to face and solve problems. Life often presents a series of challenges and problems that must be addressed. Each time we meet a challenge, we grow. Even failures can teach us valuable lessons that help us mature. Avoiding these challenges and lessons will keep us stagnant.

Substance abusers are avoidance pros. Instead of trying to deal with life and its pain and hardships, they escape through the use of mind-altering substances. When they're doing poorly in school, they use drugs. When they feel abandoned by their parents, they get drunk. When they lose their job, they get high. When they feel bored, they get stoned. When they feel angry at the world, they get blotto. Instead of facing an issue, perhaps asking for help and trying to find a solution, they disappear through their chemical escape hatch. This keeps them perpetually immature and unable to cope with life in any constructive way.

When families help addicts avoid the consequences of their actions—which might be losing their home or job, going hungry, going to jail—the families are depriving addicts of an opportunity to grow. Likewise, when families are able to step back and let events follow the natural course, they are giving their loved ones a chance to learn valuable lessons. The phrase *growing pains* comes to mind here, reminding us that human growth often involves some pain. By letting their loved ones feel the pain of addiction, families are leaving the door to recovery wide open.

Don't Enable

The distinction between helping and enabling usually causes families much confusion. Enabling, as the word is used in the treatment community, is any action that in any way makes it easier for the addict to continue using. Some family members define it as doing for the addicts what they can and should be doing for themselves. For example, loaning an active addict twenty dollars is a clear case of enabling. In this case, the loan will make it easier for the addict to purchase drugs. Paying an addict's bills is enabling. Lying and covering up for the addict is enabling. Often it is easy to identify an enabling act, even though it is not always easy to prevent ourselves from doing it. At other times, enabling is not so easy to spot.

What, for example, are parents to do if their daughter has no food in her house because she has spent her money on drugs? Surely buying her groceries is not enabling. The question becomes even more complicated if there are grandchildren involved. How can the parents not pay the rent, buy the food, and pay the heating bill when innocent children might suffer? Is it enabling to rescue a sick and hurting person from living on the streets?

The sad truth is that anytime we do anything to prevent our addicted loved ones from fully experiencing the consequences of their actions, we are enabling to some extent. I was aware of this when I let my daughter continue living with me even after she broke my rule of not using drugs in my house. I was aware of this when I signed for her second and third car loans. I was aware of this when I put gas in her car and gave her money for cigarettes.

These decisions were based on my evaluation of the situation and my own sense of what I could live with. She was working, she paid her bills, she was going to counseling and Twelve Step meetings, and she was, most often, respectful of me. Since she was making at least some effort to get better, I did not feel it was wrong to offer her help in these ways. I also felt I could not live with myself if I didn't at least know that she had a roof over her head at night. However, since my efforts, in some circumstances, made her using easier, I, too, was guilty of enabling.

Like me, most families struggle to define the line between helping and enabling. (Even families who aren't dealing with addiction problems may sometimes question whether giving a child money for gas is helping him or her avoid learning financial responsibility.) Sometimes recognizing the difference between helping and enabling forces families to make painful decisions. To offer a helping hand to a family member in need is normal. Unfortunately, it is also normal for addicts to prey on family members who want to help.

Family members have to evaluate the situation for themselves and ask whether their actions are supporting addiction or supporting recovery and then follow their own conscience. Talking to a sponsor in Al-Anon, friend, therapist, or clergy member informed about addiction can help the family member decide.

Don't Scold, Criticize, Shame, or Reject
Many addicted people feel a great deal of self-loathing. Often these negative feelings prolong their addiction. Sometimes families hope that if addicts feel bad enough about themselves, they will want to change. The opposite is usually true. As Lia explained it, "If somebody gives you tons of stuff, that's enabling. If someone just ditches you, that just makes you go out there and use."

I remember ranting at my daughter one night, saying

something like, "What's the matter with you? Can't you see what you're doing to yourself? Can't you learn from your mistakes?" I later asked Mark, a recovering alcoholic, what he thought about such tactics. He said, "If someone said that to me, I'd think, 'I guess I can't learn from my mistakes. I guess I'm just stupid. I might as well go have a drink.'"

Making people feel bad about themselves is never an effective way to encourage them to change. Instead it makes them discouraged and hostile. If families are seething with anger (which at times they may well be) or filled with frustration (which is almost inevitable), they need to process these emotions in a healthy venue so they don't do damage to themselves or to their addicted loved ones. Counseling *can* help. It's also helpful to remember a rule of thumb heard in Twelve Step meetings: "If you can't help an addict, at least don't hurt him."

Jane feels grateful for the way her mother handled her years of active addiction. "My mother was devastated. She drew the line and refused to rescue me. But she wasn't mean about it," she said. "She calmly told my kids it was drugs. 'Your mother is very sick, but maybe someday she'll find her way back,' she said to them. Her kindness helped a lot when I was finally ready to get better."

A subtle but not harmless form of criticism occurs when we consistently try to exert our control over our loved ones. When we tell them to call their counselor, inquire about a job, or get the oil changed on their car, we are saying we don't think they're bright or capable enough to consider these things themselves. They may well have proven to us that they won't do these things on their own, but nothing can be gained, and much can be lost, by assuming their responsibilities. When people do things because we told them to, we have deprived them of the satisfaction of solving a problem on their own and given them an opportunity to blame us for the outcome. Thus controlling perpetuates the very immaturity that we would like our loved ones to overcome.

Often our attempts to control are disguised as encouragement, such as when we suggest that they could do so much more with their lives or look so much better if they dressed or wore their hair a certain way. When we tell others how they should live or act, we are telling them they are not good enough as they are. (Isn't that what we really think about our addicted loved ones—that they are not good enough?)

A counselor pointed this out to me when I said of my daughter, before her addiction problems fully blossomed, "She has so much potential. She could do so much." The counselor said, "When you say that to her, she doesn't hear encouragement. She hears criticism of who she is now. She hears she's not good enough." Of course, I did want her to change the direction of her life, but my clumsy efforts to control her choices were actually doing more harm than good. I had yet to learn the difference between encouragement and criticism.

Be Consistent
Addicts live in a shifting world of lies, deception, and self-delusion. They are experts at twisting the truth and at convincing themselves (and often their families) of the validity of their misperceptions. Everyday reality can become ill-defined, even nonexistent, to clouded minds. Yet if addicts are to recover, they must learn to function within the common boundaries of society, to find their place in the world of every day. Families can help by creating an environment that is consistent, dependable, and grounded.

This can be hard to do when families themselves are floundering in the mire of addictive behaviors. Nothing has prepared most families for dealing with the irrational, often bizarre, world of addiction, and it is easy to get caught up in destructive patterns without even realizing it. Yet many families have found the following four tactics helpful for promoting normalcy and building consistency into their relationships with their addicted loved ones.

First, avoid setting unreasonable ultimatums and inappropriate consequences, especially for minor children. Threatening to throw a child out for "taking one more drink" is an example of such behavior. Following through on this threat would be punitive and unhelpful, and failing to follow through would undermine the parent's authority. (Making idle threats is a bad strategy in any relationship.) Although families may have to establish rules and consequences, they should do so in moments of clarity, not in anger. Professional guidance can be helpful in setting realistic guidelines that families can live with.

Second, "Say what you mean and mean what you say, but don't say it mean." This advice, often heard in Twelve Step meetings, addresses the communication problems inherent in any relationship with an addicted person. Talking to an addict can feel like walking on eggshells.

To me, talking to my daughter felt more like tiptoeing through a minefield. I never knew what benign remark might set off a bout of tears, rage, hysteria, or stony silence. I hesitated to say, "Your bathroom is a mess" or, "Your clothes are all over the house" or, "You burned holes in my blankets." I found it almost impossible to talk about my core concern: her addiction and recovery. Intimidated by her instability, I lived for long periods in an uneasy truce with her during which neither of us talked about what was on our minds. This state of affairs felt dishonest to me, and I worried that she thought she was keeping her drug use hidden from me or—worse—that I didn't care about the status of her recovery efforts.

Gradually, with the help of a counselor, I learned that I had a right to express my feelings regardless of what her reactions might be. I learned to make "I" statements, such as "I don't like it when you make a mess of my stuff" or "I'm concerned about you, and I'd like to know how things are going." I might say, "I worry when I don't hear from you" or, "I won't sign for another loan for you. I told you that, and I meant it." I also learned to sort through the complexity of conflicting thoughts in my head by asking myself, "Do I want to say something because I think that doing so will change her, or do I want to say it because that's how I honestly feel?" By consciously examining my motives, I learned to reduce some of the chaos in our household. By speaking honestly with no ulterior motive other than to express our feelings, we lay the foundation for open communication and set a tone of truthfulness, both important elements of anyone's recovery.

Third, remind yourself, "You don't have to go to every battle you're invited to." Another gem heard in Twelve Step meetings, this saying hints at the emotional upheaval wrought by addiction. Addicts give us lots of opportunities to get worked up. They break their promises, don't follow through on commitments, deceive and mislead us, and do their best to manipulate us into giving them what they want. If we react to everything they say or do, our lives would be permanent chaos. This type of reacting does nobody, including addicts, any good. We can create a saner, less fractious relationship with our loved ones by learning to avoid unnecessary conflicts.

One man recalled, "My daughter knew how to push my buttons. We were always at each other's throats until I figured out that I didn't have to react to everything she said or did. I could walk away. Sometimes I'd even get in my car and go for a drive rather than listen to her nonsense."

Evading troubling issues simply to avoid a confrontation or crisis isn't helpful. However, neither is it helpful or useful to react to every problem that presents itself. Learning to overlook the small things helps us find the emotional energy to deal rationally and consistently with the core issues that must be addressed.

Fourth and finally, get honest about your own substance issues. Many counselors point out that when someone has an addiction problem, frequently other substance use may be going on within the family. One teenager exclaimed angrily to his parents during a therapy session, "Why are you busting my balls? The two of you smoke pot every night!" I struggled with this issue myself after my daughter came home. I often had a glass of beer or wine in the evening, yet I wanted her to be abstinent. Did that mean I had to give up my small pleasures? Unfortunately, yes. That glass of beer was not more important than my being a model of abstinence for her. I began practicing what I was preaching.

Counselors advise that, in the grand scheme of things, it is helpful to establish a dry household while someone is in the early days of recovery. For the alcoholic in the family, seeing others drink can be a trigger. While recovering addicts and alcoholics must learn to be abstinent in a world in which alcohol and other substances are plentiful, establishing a dry household, even for a short time, can underscore the message that substance abuse is not acceptable. As is always the case, our example is stronger when our actions match our words.

Encourage the Addict to Get Treatment

Addiction is a disease of the body, mind, and spirit, a complex malady that makes its victims cling to the source of their own misery. Although some individuals are able to overcome addiction solely through a fortuitous combination of character and circumstance, most addicted people require some form of intervention or treatment to guide and support their recovery efforts.

Families cannot force their loved one to get help, except in the case of minor children. But they can provide information, such as phone numbers of social service agencies or lists of AA or NA meetings. They can say such things as "I'm concerned. I know there are people who can help you" and back up their words with an offer to help their loved one make the appropriate connections. They can sometimes make appointments for their loved one and take their loved one to meetings. Families should not, however, take on the addict's responsibility for developing and maintaining an effective support network. Above all, family members should not nag.

The question of how much effort families should put into getting their loved one into treatment is hard to answer. After all, we don't want to be controlling. Responsibility for recovery from addiction rests squarely on the shoulders of the addict. As one detox center employee caustically pointed out to me, "Your daughter didn't need your help to find drugs. She doesn't need your help to find recovery." Yet I *wanted* her to get help. She seemed receptive, so I made the initial contact with an agency and took her to an intake meeting. I also made regular counseling sessions and participation in Twelve Step meetings conditions of her being allowed to live with me.

At one point, she tried to get out of the counseling by faking her counselor's signature on appointment cards. And she most likely didn't go to even half the NA meetings she claimed she was attending. But more important, she learned that help was available, and she gained knowledge and support both from her counselor and from members of NA.

Looking back, I can see that I was successful in introducing my daughter to treatment because she was in a vulnerable state. She was friendless, homeless, and penniless, forced by circumstances to consider the consequences of her drug problems. Frequently, when substance abusers are in a similar condition, they feel vulnerable, remorseful, or depressed. Then they are most receptive to the suggestion that they seek help. It is almost always a waste of time to try to convince people who are under the influence of alcohol or other drugs that they need help. But when the high is worn off, when the addict is again enduring the bleak aftermath of intoxication, family members have an opportunity to encourage their loved one to get help and to propose some treatment options. Among those options are Twelve Step programs, individual counseling, and inpatient or outpatient care in a specialized facility.

For many addicted individuals, Twelve Step programs become the backbone of recovery. The meetings provide a wonderful source of support, encouragement, and hope and are absolutely free and available almost everywhere in the world. Alcohol and other drug users can attend whatever meetings are most comfortable for them, whether Alcoholics Anonymous, Narcotics Anonymous, or other Twelve Step programs. The principles and the meeting procedures are identical. Furthermore, although the programs are based on spiritual principles of humility and self-knowledge, they are not religious. Members are free to believe whatever they wish. Also worth noting is that addicts need not be clean or sober to attend meetings. They need only be willing to listen or have a desire to stop using.

Twelve Step programs are truly a gift to the world, offering the opportunity to share deep personal feelings on a level that is rarely experienced elsewhere in our society. These meetings can be invaluable in helping addicts and family members overcome their sense of isolation, their commonly held belief that they are fundamentally unique and set apart from others. In meetings, addicts and family members learn that others have faced and solved similar problems. They experience an environment of acceptance and understanding. And they meet individuals who are solemnly aware that the quality of their lives depends on remaining clean and sober, that they are engaged in a life-and-death struggle, and that their commitment to staying well must be absolute. Although not everyone in recovery embraces Twelve Step programs, attending even a few meetings can be extremely beneficial to most addicts and family members.

Professional treatment, unlike Twelve Step programs, may be based on a variety of philosophies. It includes inpatient hospitalization, outpatient care, and individual counseling. Many treatment centers offer programs for family members of addicts as well. Not all treatment is equal, and not all treatment is appropriate for every individual. For example, minor children and other dependent youths should receive help from professionals who specialize in treating young people. The individuals involved must decide for themselves which type of treatment fits them best.

Finding appropriate treatment is especially critical for individuals with co-occurring disorders. As is mentioned in chapter 3, the National Co-Morbidity Survey, which was headed by Dr. Robert Kessler in the early 1990s, indicates that about ten million adults in our country suffer from at least one mental health disorder and one substance abuse disorder. Frequently, the people with co-occurring disorders are isolated, with few, if any, friends they can rely on. In the words of Bert Pepper, M.D., in *Blamed and Ashamed:*

> The person with mental health and alcohol and other drug abuse problems may experience their drug of choice as their best friend; it seems to fill the emptiness

in their heart. Beginning drug abuse treatment, which requires or involves abstinence, may lead to feeling much worse. The "best friend" is gone, and the emptiness within is devastating. For this reason, substance abuse programs must address loneliness, sadness, the sense of loss, and the depression that often accompanies early recovery. Otherwise, the person may be motivated to leave treatment and rush back to drug or alcohol use, because they cannot bear their depression and loneliness. (p. 53)

Historically, there have been four treatment options for these people: no treatment, drug treatment only, mental health treatment only, and parallel treatment in which the patient receives services for addiction and mental health issues separately, not simultaneously. Today, more centers offer integrated treatment. With this approach the patient receives treatment for addiction and mental health problems from one team of providers from varied backgrounds who are cross-trained to work together. Clients' addiction issues are addressed along with their underlying emotional issues so that one issue is not viewed as less significant than the other. Of course, not everything can be accomplished at once, and abstinence may be an early goal in the treatment process. The long-term goal is to move the client away from addiction and into a condition of improved mental health.

A 1999 booklet produced by the National Institute on Drug Abuse, *Principles of Drug Addiction Treatment*, endorses integrated treatment, stating, "Addicted or drug abusing individuals with co-existing mental disorders should have both disorders treated in an integrated way." Although integrated treatment is not yet widely available, it is worth seeking out for those individuals suffering from co-occurring disorders.

However, keep in mind that treatment is not a cure for

addiction. As the National Institute on Drug Abuse also states in its 1999 booklet, "Recovery from drug addiction can be a long-term process and frequently requires multiple episodes of treatment." In other words, treatment may not bring about desired changes the first, second, or even third time around. Nevertheless, these attempts are important steps toward recovery, and families should make an effort to encourage their loved one to get help.

Practice Intervention
Many addicted individuals are resistant to the idea of getting help. They insist they are okay, that they can quit anytime, or that the family is making a big deal out of nothing. Denial is the nature of the disease of addiction. Although an addicted person's own experiences may eventually lead him or her to seek help, sometimes intervention is necessary.

Broadly speaking, interventions are acts that arrest the progression of substance abuse, that mark a turning point from active addiction toward recovery. Interventions can be informal, often unplanned, occurrences or formally planned events. Getting arrested for driving while intoxicated, being involuntarily committed to a mental health facility, and going to jail are all examples of informal interventions. Addicted individuals may not get better after such experiences—they may even get worse—but at the very least these events disrupt the pattern of addictive behavior and can potentially alert them to the consequences of their use.

Less dramatic informal interventions also occur. A recovering alcoholic remembered a friend saying, "I have observed that your drinking is causing problems." Although he heard little else that she had to say, that remark stayed with him. It raised his level of awareness, and he eventually sought recovery. Another man stopped drinking after ash from his cigarette fell and burned a hole in a $150 pair of pants. "I was used to taking from six to twelve drinks a day, but I never touched another drop after that happened," he recalled.

Simply changing a routine can also interrupt a substance-abuse pattern. A counselor related the story of how some boys in a group home would pool their weekly allowance and buy large quantities of pot and alcohol on the weekend. Several ended up in the hospital with alcohol poisoning. Since the allowance was state mandated, counselors could not withhold it. Instead, they moved allowance time from Friday afternoons to Monday mornings. By the time weekends came, most of the money had been spent on candy and other incidentals. "By disrupting the pattern, reorganizing it, we got a different outcome," the counselor said. "We never had the problem with substances again." He added that the home also provided counseling and education as part of a larger plan of intervention.

Small interventions happen whenever something occurs that disrupts the usual pattern of addictive thoughts and be-haviors. In a sense, families are doing small interventions when they stop engaging in unhealthy interactions, such as nagging or blaming their addicted loved one, and begin intro-ducing healthier ways of dealing with issues.

Larger, planned interventions are carefully orchestrated events designed to bring about abstinence and recovery. Although they can be quite effective, they can also be counter-productive if the addicted individual feels ridiculed, hu-miliated, chastised, or rejected. Planned interventions are best done with assistance from a substance abuse treatment professional.

In general, formal interventions consist of several steps. First, an organizer recruits concerned friends and family members to participate in the event. The organizer or professional facilitator also makes arrangements with a treatment facility so the addicted individual can go directly from the intervention into treatment.

Second, each participant writes a letter that expresses affection, concern, and clear, specific observations about the negative impact of substances on the individual's life. It is important that concrete examples of negative behaviors be given and not ones such as "You've become insensitive," "You've let yourself go," or "You've gained a lot of weight."

Third, because emotions will usually run high during an intervention, participants read their letters out loud during a rehearsal. This helps them maintain a tone of objectivity during the actual event.

Fourth, participants gather at a meeting place, taking the target of the intervention by surprise and at a time when the individual is not likely to be under the influence of alcohol or other drugs.

Fifth, with the guidance of a professional facilitator, participants read their letters, taking care to maintain a tone of love and concern.

Finally, the addicted individual is informed that treatment has been arranged and is urged to enter the treatment facility. These six steps are a much abbreviated version of a intervention. Calling a professional interventionist or reading about interventions can add valuable information. Such an event may sound scary to some, but interventions are really an opportunity for family members to express their love and concern for their addicted loved one.

Peter was in his early thirties when he decided to arrange a formal intervention for his father. He explained, "Dad's drinking had been a problem for years. My mother and he had the classic codependent relationship where he would drink and she would nag. I was after him all the time too. It

was almost like a game in that he'd try to outsmart us by
sneaking drinks when he thought we wouldn't notice. After
[Mom] died, he got worse. He'd be drinking by nine in the
morning, and he got all bloated and the blood vessels in his
face began to break. He'd been very successful in his career,
but he began having a lot of problems at work. My worry
about him was also causing a lot of problems in my own life. I
decided to organize an intervention as a last resort. I thought
of it as my final effort to help him. If it didn't work and he insisted on drinking himself to death, I would at least know I'd
tried everything I could."

Peter called in a professional to help. He recalled the following from the intervention: "Dad sat there smoking a cigarette, looking at each person in turn without a word or flicker
of expression. After we'd all read our letters he said, 'Where
do I go?' We had arranged for a stay in a residential facility,
and after that he went into a day program. He's been sober
ever since and is doing consulting work and traveling a bit.
Looking back, my impression of him during the intervention
was of a little kid who finally realizes that all these people love
him. He finally got the attention he'd always wanted."

Lynn is a recovering alcoholic who was on the receiving
end of an intervention organized without professional assistance. She recalled, "I was an active alcoholic for about four
years. Through this period I alienated many, many people. I
was totally obnoxious when I was drunk. I was also an impossible mother, and my son and I had what surely must have
been one of the worst relationships in the history of parenthood. Fortunately for me, I also had many friends who
responded with love rather than censure. They did an intervention on me, and it was a dreadful experience. I was horri-
fied. I resented everyone terribly at the same time that I
recognized their love and concern."

She continued, "The intervention was not what turned the tide. Instead, it was one friend who was there. He knew that the intervention hadn't had the effect that they all had hoped for. So he followed up. He arrived at my door one morning and walked me down to an outpatient alcohol-abatement service. It ran every weekday from 4:00 to 9:00 P.M. for five weeks. I signed up, and that was what did the trick. Oddly enough, once my head was pointed in that direction, quitting drinking was easy, and the behaviors fell away like so much rain. I think interventions can be helpful, but I believe follow-up is necessary."

Whether small or large, formal or informal, interventions can be effective tools for helping addicted individuals see their situation in a new light. They are most successful when combined with a wide range of strategies aimed at promoting recovery for the addicts and their families.

PROMOTING THE RECOVERY OF FAMILY MEMBERS

Basically, a family's search for recovery is nothing more than a search for peace of mind. Yet many families feel guilty about seeking recovery for themselves. They ask, "How can we try to live a more serene life when our loved one is suffering so terribly?" or, "What right do we have to happiness when this person we love is falling apart?" In truth, it is hard to imagine that the family's stone of despair can be lifted until the addiction has been overcome. Most families say to themselves, "First the addiction must be addressed; only then can we begin to live normal lives again."

Unfortunately, recovery rarely seems to happen that way. In my experience, and in the experience of most people I have talked with, the family's recovery often coincides with or precedes the recovery of the addicted individual. This is probably because families in recovery are learning to avoid destructive patterns that may actually prolong or, as discussed earlier, enable addiction. They become more likely to engage in emotionally healthy behaviors that benefit themselves and those they love, including the addict. And they are developing coping skills that enable them to deal with turmoil in ways that may promote healing, both for themselves and for their addicted loved one.

Families in recovery recognize that while no one can guarantee that their own recovery will help their loved one overcome addiction, no evidence exists to suggest that their prolonged misery is of any benefit to anyone. They rediscover the simple truth that their own lives have value—*independent* of the status of their loved one's addiction problems.

Although all come to recovery only in their own time and in their own way, certain guidelines seem to ease the process of recovering from the impact of addiction. These guidelines have helped many families as they struggled to find a way out of the maze of despair. They are not meant to be a road map but rather to serve as guideposts along the unfolding journey of recovery.

Get Support

Few experiences can equal the heartbreak of watching someone you love being destroyed by alcohol or other drugs. The emotional impact can be devastating, yet the tendency of many families is to isolate and keep their suffering to themselves. After all, addiction is a disease of secrets, and families are often all too willing to join their loved one in the game of concealment.

For many, the first step along the path of recovery is reaching out for support. Although this may seem like an obvious place to start, it is actually a huge step. It requires admitting that a problem exists. Families who have denied and mini-mized the difficulties caused by substance abuse crack open the door to change when they become willing to ask for help.

Finding the right support can begin by sharing the prob-lem with someone we trust, such as a close friend or relative who will lend a sympathetic ear. Confidants should be people who can listen without judging and who do not bombard us with unwelcome advice that will only further confuse things. One father of an alcoholic daughter recalled that his close friends were sympathetic about the situation except for one who advised, "Put your foot down. She wouldn't get away with that in my house." The father said, "We learned who we could talk to and who we couldn't. People who don't under-stand the problem can say foolish things, but most of our close friends have been very supportive. They ask how she's doing. They care about our daughter, and that makes it a bit easier for us." Getting support from friends and family can help reduce the sense of isolation and despair.

Support can also come from self-help groups, including Al-Anon and Nar-Anon. These Twelve Step programs are de-signed to support families of substance abusers, and they promote understanding and personal growth. I began attend-ing Nar-Anon meetings soon after learning of my daughter's addiction, motivated by the desire to discover a way to "fix" her. What I found instead was a group of fellow sufferers who had endured the same fears, sorrow, and frustration that I was experiencing. They had faced the same despair and learned to live their lives with hope and grace. It was in those meetings that I learned that I am not a bad person because my daughter had become addicted, that I am not the only one who had endured years of grinding anxiety, that other people have learned to enjoy life again despite a loved one's addic-tion, and (miracle of miracles!) that some families have expe-rienced the joy of seeing their loved one recover.

In those meetings, I found the hope that my own daughter would one day become one of those miracles. For me and others coping with addiction, self-help groups have become a lifeline of comfort and support. Be aware that personalities can have a powerful impact on group dynamics. If you give a group a chance but do not find it compatible with your needs, feel free to try other groups until you find one that fits. Although friends and family can offer support, they can't offer the comfort that comes only from those who have walked in your shoes.

Another important source of support is professional counseling. This is almost always useful because families of addicts are in distress. They are dealing with something for which they are usually not prepared, and family dynamics are often strained. Guilt, blame, shame, resentment, fear, and other intense emotions can run high, creating an unhappy atmosphere. Depression and anger are common. Counselors experienced in substance abuse can help families work through their emotions in a constructive way and provide a framework for coping with inevitable issues. Even if the addicted person or other family members are not willing to accept professional assistance, the situation can improve when even one family member gets help.

Detach with Love

When I was first advised to detach from my daughter's problems, I thought I was being told to turn my back on her. Putting space between my daughter and me felt like setting her adrift on an angry sea. It felt unnatural, heartless, and just plain wrong. After all, how could I not be involved in the problems of someone I loved so much? How could I not be ready to jump in and help the moment she needed me? I thought it was inhuman to think otherwise.

Like many family members, I was confused about the true nature of detachment. It seemed at best a convenient label for shirking responsibility and at worst a cruel act of outright abandonment. It took me a long time to understand that detachment has nothing to do with rejection or abandonment, that it is neither kind nor unkind, that it is simply a way for individuals to reestablish the distinction between themselves and their addicted loved one.

When family members become wrapped up in their loved one's problems, they can lose their sense of self. They begin to suffer along with—and in some instances *instead of*—the addict, experiencing every jolt and crisis as intensely as if the addict's problems were their own. Unhappiness, anxiety, and depression are the result of experiencing the pain of addiction while being powerless to arrest or control the problem. Families live at the mercy of the addict, to whom they have subjugated their own identity.

This unhealthy situation can begin to improve only when families detach from their addicted loved one and once again become independent, freethinking individuals. When we detach, we learn to respond to crises with such comments as "I'm sorry to hear it. I'm sure you'll figure something out," "I know you're a capable person. You can handle this on your own," and "That's too bad." When we detach, we don't rush in to fix everything but rather allow other people to solve their problems themselves. We also learn to protect ourselves by not getting drawn into conflict.

One mother said that her most useful tool for dealing with a manipulative addicted daughter was simply the word *oh.* "When she told me something I didn't believe or that upset me, I learned I didn't have to pry or react. I could just say oh and leave it at that," she explained. By refusing to engage in crises and conflicts, we are not being callous or indifferent. We are simply respecting ourselves enough to live our own lives and respecting our loved ones enough to let them live theirs.

At first detachment is hard. It feels like loss. It feels like failure. It is neither. It is a simple recognition that the addict's problems and struggle are not our problems and struggle. We can offer support, encouragement, and love, but we cannot live another person's life, only our own.

Let Go

Letting go of certain behaviors and attitudes can greatly increase our peace of mind, especially letting go of the need to control, letting go of passing judgment, and letting go of expectations.

Families want to control their addicted loved one because they want to save him or her. Addiction destroys lives. Addiction kills. These facts haunt and terrify families, making them want to take charge of their loved one completely. It can't be done, but concerned families do not give up easily. The harder they try to control things, the more stressful their situation is likely to become. Families may also cling to control because they are hooked on their own sense of power and the mistaken belief that they are the only ones who can "fix" the addiction.

"I thought that through the power of my love, wisdom, and will, I could make him give up drugs," one wife admitted.

A husband said, "I wanted her to get well, but I wanted to be the one to make it happen."

The urge to control is further heightened by the desire to escape the all-consuming anxiety that addiction can bring. If we can control the problem, we can fix it, and then we won't have to feel so awful. The sad truth is that we can't control our loved one's life, and we can't control addiction. Furthermore, trying to exert control does the addict no good and only brings unhappiness and frustration to ourselves. Letting go of control is hard because we fear that things will fall apart without our interference. It helps to recognize that our efforts to control have not solved anything. It helps to remember that there are many people and events exerting influence over our loved one, and we have no way of knowing when or how circumstances will come together to bring about the miracle of recovery. It also helps to have hope that our loved one's recovery will happen in its own way and to accept that it will most likely *not* happen as a result of our efforts to take control.

Families are often tempted to pass harsh judgments on their addicted loved ones. They want to size up the status of any recovery efforts ("He's not doing so well," "Her attitude is getting in the way," or "She's not making progress as fast as she should"). They may be highly critical if a slip or relapse occurs. But when we place ourselves in a position of judgment over others, we are judging based only on what we *believe* we know of them. In reality, we do not know how many times they may have turned down an opportunity to get high before they gave in to temptation. We do not know the internal workings of their minds, fears, desires, or intentions.

Even though a judgmental attitude generally stems from an anxious desire to see the addict recover, it almost always results in conflict and unhappiness. When we can see a particular occurrence as just another step in the process of change, we free ourselves from the burden of worry that things are not as they ought to be. When we can look at our addicted loved one and see a fellow human being who is trying for better or worse to cope with life in the best way possible at any particular moment, then the peace of acceptance can flow into our lives.

Letting go of expectations is fundamental to recovery for most families. Only then can we stop projecting and worrying about the outcome of things. We should also not expect that people will or won't behave in a particular way. Many of us live on a roller coaster of hope and disappointment, fear and relief, as we try to predict what the future will bring to our addicted loved one. We pace the floor at night fearing that the worst has happened, we're flooded with happiness as a new attempt at abstinence is made, or we knot up in tension as something else goes wrong. Although emotional highs and lows are an inevitable part of coping with addiction, most of us aggravate and intensify our feelings by setting up expectations.

"I used to lie awake at night picturing my daughter dead in a Dumpster," one mother confessed. "Today, she's a computer technician and engaged to a wonderful guy who's also in recovery."

"I turned against an old friend because she didn't react the way I hoped she would when I told her about my son's addiction," another woman said. "Now I see that she wasn't wrong. I was wrong to expect that she would react just the way I wanted."

A father said, "I always wanted a preppy son, and what I got was a kid with piercings, tattoos, and a serious drug problem. I love him anyway, but to arrive at unconditional love, I had to let go of a lot of expectations."

Letting go of expecting that people should live up to our standards and of projecting that things will or won't turn out as we hope allow us to live more consciously in the present. When we let go of fears about the future or disappointment because our expectations haven't been met, we are better able to appreciate what is good in the here and now.

Set Boundaries

No one will test your boundaries like a habitual substance abuser. Because we worry about them and know that they are sick and suffering, we tend for a time to accept behaviors in our addicted loved ones that would be intolerable in anyone else. Most families, to a greater or lesser degree, accept lies, irresponsibility, and disrespect from their addicts. Some accept stealing, cheating, and destruction of property. Others accept verbal and even physical abuse. We accept these behaviors not because we are blind or weak, but because we believe that the addicts are somehow not responsible. "It is the drink or the drug that is doing this," we rationalize.

We also accept these behaviors because we don't want to drive the addicts away and because we fear that standing up for ourselves will only make the addiction worse. If we don't upset them, we reason, they will have less reason to go out for another drink or fix. The problem with this approach is that addicts have no limits. That's how they became addicted in the first place. Each time we allow them to cross a line, they will cross it again and again. Eventually we can end up feeling like there is no place in our home or mind or soul that we can call our own. If we are to have a life of our own, we will have to draw the line.

I drew one line with my daughter because of her lapses into hysteria whenever she was faced with a crisis. Whenever she'd freak out, I'd get upset and devise a rescue plan. After about a year of this, I'd had enough. One day we were standing in the kitchen, and she was screaming and crying about some major or minor problem. I looked at her coldly and said, "I find your hysterical behavior irritating and manipulative. It doesn't make me feel sorry for you. It just annoys me. So stop it." She quickly got herself under control and as far as I can recall, she never expressed herself that way again.

Another woman drew the line at having syringes in her home. "Our daughter used pot and alcohol, and we were living with that because we thought we could help her," she recalled. "But when we started finding needles and drug paraphernalia in the house, we asked her to leave. We have other children at home, and we just couldn't tolerate that."

The wife of an alcoholic said, "I put up with his lies and his absence from home for days at a time. When he started stealing money out of my purse, I realized we didn't have a relationship anymore. He was just using me. I told him to leave, and I've never regretted it."

Addicts, like most people, do what works and what they can get away with. Sometimes people in the throes of active addiction can't prevent themselves from crossing boundaries. That is *their* problem to work on and solve as best they can. Our problem is to decide what we can and can't live with, to make our boundaries clear, and to take whatever steps are necessary to preserve our safety and sense of self-respect.

Focus on Yourself

Of all the recovery tools for families of addicts, perhaps none presents a greater challenge than focusing on ourselves. This may be because it feels selfish to put ourselves first when we are used to taking care of others. It may also be because many of us don't know who our "self" is anymore.

"When people told me to focus on myself, I thought they were nuts," one woman exclaimed. "I didn't know who I was, so there was nothing for me to focus on unless I was looking after my son."

Another woman said that she had abandoned all of her interests over the years as she became increasingly preoccupied with her son's substance abuse problems. "I used to love to do crafts and sewing," she said. "I made some beautiful things. But I stopped all that when his problems started."

A father said, "I didn't even know what I believed in or stood for, because I'd spent so much time covering up and making excuses for my daughter."

For many of us, focusing on ourselves is a process of discovering what we feel, what we enjoy, and what we believe in. It may mean pursuing interests that can help us grow spiritually, intellectually, and emotionally. It may mean trying new activities, meeting new people, and learning new things. It may mean reconnecting with people and things we enjoyed but abandoned over the years.

Whatever direction focusing on ourselves takes us, it can, at first, be extremely uncomfortable. We may experience turbulent emotions, such as anger, resentment, and guilt if we have buried our emotions in concern about the addict. We may experience a sense of emptiness if we have directed all our energies to trying to help the addict. We may also feel oddly disoriented because it is much easier to see how others should live their lives than it is to see how we should live our own. Yet our own life is the only one that we truly have to work with, the only one that is absolutely ours to control. It is a gift and no less precious, no less valuable, than the life of our addicted loved one. When we put the focus on ourselves, we are not turning our back on others in need or giving up on our responsibility to someone we love. We are simply choosing to cherish this one life that is ours and to live it to the very best of our ability.

A JOURNEY, NOT A DESTINATION

To follow a path of recovery is to embrace the concept that growth and change are a natural part of life. There is never a point when we can say we are fully recovered, that the process is complete. For addicts and their families, a life in recovery reveals endless new challenges, insights, strengths, and possibilities. One special reward of recovery is the opportunity to heal our wounds, to emerge with some degree of wisdom and serenity from the crucible of addiction.

In the next chapter we will look at what the process of healing can mean.

SEVEN

TIME TO HEAL

Years ago, one fine spring morning, Jane dropped off her two small children at their baby-sitter's house. Then she went home and, with her boyfriend, loaded all her household possessions into a U-Haul truck. The drug-addicted couple was bound for Florida, and although they didn't get far, that act of abandonment initiated eight years of estrangement between Jane and her children. During that painful period, the children lived with their grandparents as their mother sank ever deeper into a life of rehabs, relapses, and imprisonment. What confusion, hurt, and sorrow the children endured can well be imagined, as can their mother's shame, guilt, and bitter sense of loss.

Yet after eight years of being drug- and alcohol-free, Jane recently spent a vacation in Hawaii with her children—a family getaway that included her son and daughter-in-law and her daughter and her daughter's boyfriend. The family spent nine days sightseeing, relaxing on the beach, and talking and playing together.

"It's a miracle," said Jane, who once survived a frigid winter by sleeping in cellars. "My life today is truly a miracle. Not that everything is perfect. My daughter still has a lot of anger at me. The hurt is still there, even though a lot of healing has taken place."

Jane's relationship with her mother is beginning to heal as well. She explained, "My parents disowned me during those years. When I got my first-year coin [awarded by AA for being substance free], my mother just said, 'That's good. Get one next year.' The second year it was the same thing because she was afraid to trust. But the third year she went to my meeting with me and gave me my coin. And my sister just gave me my eight-year coin." She paused and added, "Healing takes time. I think it's a lifelong process."

Jack, a recovering alcoholic and father of a recovering addict, echoed that sentiment. "Healing is ongoing," he said. "We haven't 'arrived.' It's not a place where you go and everything's all better. I still make mistakes. I still have bad days. Everybody does. But I also have peace, and that's what healing is all about for me. Making peace with the past and being able to appreciate the present."

His words capture the essence of the concept of healing: being able to appreciate what is good and beautiful in life even as we acknowledge the presence of suffering, putting things to rest piece by piece, and attaining a sustaining measure of inner peace. A serene state of mind can seem unattainable to families who are embroiled in the trauma of active addiction. Even when families are actively seeking their own recovery, they may wonder why things don't seem to get better. They may practice detachment, set personal boundaries, build a network of support, and try to develop their own individual interests—yet they may still be burdened with a host of unhappy feelings including anxiety, sadness, guilt, anger, resentment, and shame. They may still feel the pain of addiction dragging them down.

The truth is that the tools of recovery can open the door

to a better way of life, but the real miracle of healing is almost always a slow process.

CHOOSING TO HEAL

Addiction cuts deep into the fabric of family relationships. Trust is broken. Expectations are shattered. The accumulation of worry, disappointment, and heartache takes its toll. It is not uncommon for family members to wonder if they will ever be capable of experiencing happiness again.

Hope, whose daughter repeatedly broke her heart, said, "For years I felt dead inside. I thought of myself as a flower that had withered away and died. Only very gradually did I come to see that I could continue to wallow in my pain or I could choose to begin the healing process. I had to heal if I ever wanted a better quality of life. For me, healing started when I made the choice not to be a victim but instead to be responsible for me."

As many families have found, we don't have to wait until our loved ones starts to get better before we can begin our own healing process. As Hope put it, "Healing is about *us,* not about our addicts. Our loved ones have their own journeys to make in their own time. If we really want to heal, to stop hurting inside, we have to start making choices that support our intention. We have to believe we have a right to have a happy life."

For many families, making the choice to heal includes getting involved in a Twelve Step fellowship, such as Al-Anon or Nar-Anon. One recovering spouse of an alcoholic recalled, "When I first started going to Al-Anon, I expected to find a room full of people who were miserable just like me. Instead I found people who were calm, welcoming, honest, and even happy. I wanted what they had. I decided to do whatever it took to get it, which for me meant working the program as best I could."

An active member of a Nar-Anon group said, "My daughter called us last week and said that she'd had a relapse. She's living with a guy who's actively using, and she picked up again. She cried about it, but she said she wasn't ready to try to get clean. I felt terrible after hearing the news. But I was able to sleep that night. Because I learned in this program how to make my own peace of mind a priority, I'm better able to accept whatever life brings."

Twelve Step programs have helped many families build a meaningful framework for recovery and healing, but they are not necessarily for everyone. We must all walk our own path as we strive to replace pain and suffering with hope and serenity. As we travel along that path, words of wisdom from other families who have faced addiction can help.

PRACTICING ACCEPTANCE

As families of addicts, we have devoted a lot of energy to struggling against what *is*. Simply accepting the circumstances of our lives leaves us more energy to devote to constructive activities.

Jack, whose son was addicted to crack for many years, shared his story, "I just couldn't accept that he was an addict, that he stole from me, that he was actually in prison. I mean, I knew it, but part of me couldn't accept it without being overcome by rage or grief. Part of me was always fighting against it. It took a long time before I could finally accept what had happened in our lives, before I could say, 'This is how things are. I have no choice. They are what they are.' I didn't have to like them. I didn't have to understand them. I just needed to accept them. When I finally did, I felt this great sense of calm come over me that has never completely gone away."

Families also may have to accept other previously unpalatable realities. Jack continued, "Another hard thing for me to accept was that my dreams for my son would most likely never come true. His life didn't follow the course I'd imagined it would, and I felt a real sense of loss, even betrayal, before I came to acceptance."

Hope said, "When my daughter was still using, I had to accept that I might never have a close relationship with her. I'm not sure it's possible to have a real relationship with someone who is actively using. I also had to accept the fact that she might die without being healed. That was a tough one, but it was a reality."

Deb, whose husband has struggled with addiction for years, said, "We don't fight as much as we used to. I just get sad now because this will *never* end. He will always be an addict, yet I will always love him. I sometimes grieve for the things, and the life, that I will never have. Children are quite out of the question, and sometimes that makes me sad. But I have come to accept it."

Perhaps the fundamental reality that we must come to accept is that we have control over no one's life but our own. Hope summed it up by saying, "It took me a long time to see that I alone am responsible for who I am as a person. For years I believed that if I could make someone else into the person I wanted them to be, I'd be okay. Now I see that taking care of my own life is the most I can do. And that is quite enough."

Acceptance—the antidote to denial—does not imply that change is not desirable or possible. It does not signal defeat. It is not the end of hopes and dreams. It simply means that we recognize and accept the reality of our lives as they actually exist at this moment in time.

LIVING IN THE PRESENT

It seems to be human nature to spend much of our mental existence either fretting about the past or worrying about the future. Yet many families who have healed from the effects of addiction have found that living in the present is central to their peace of mind. Living this way is hard to do, but as Deb expressed it, "I don't have power over the past or future. I only have this present moment, one day at a time. I can choose to make this day the very best I can, or choose to waste it on things over which I have no control. When I am burdened by memories, or when I start projecting about what might or might not happen tomorrow, I try to get my mind back to the here and now."

Jack said that he, too, draws strength from living in the present: "My son's clean right now, but last week he said he had a desire to use. I know that relapse could be just a moment away, but I don't let my mind go there. I work really hard to stay in the day. That's the only way I can stay healthy."

LEARNING TO FORGIVE

For most families, forgiveness is a key element of healing. As long as we harbor anger or guilt in our hearts, we are allowing ourselves to be victims of addiction. The negative feelings gnaw away at us, diminishing our capacity to fully experience what is good and worthwhile in life.

Anger is a natural response when we suffer. We look to blame someone or something for our unhappiness and end up feeling angry at the person who has caused us pain—our addicted loved one—or at society or even at God, if we have a Higher Power in our lives. Unfortunately, anger does not make us feel better. It only adds to the pain we are already feeling.

Deb recalled, "I used to get physically sick from resentment and anger. I used to feel so sorry for myself because I had married an addict and didn't have what everyone else had. Then I'd take it out on him and pick these huge fights. I really struggled with forgiveness for a long time. I still do. But I've decided that forgiving others is not a feeling. It's a decision. I can't manufacture it; it's a gift, but it starts with making the decision."

Hope, too, struggled with forgiveness. "I used to cry out to God, 'Why have you done this to me? Why have you abandoned me?' I have always been a very spiritual person. I have a strong faith. But for a long time, I was angry with God for allowing this to happen to my daughter. I was also so angry with her that I didn't talk to her for almost a year. She was in jail, and I refused to take her calls. I couldn't get past all the things she had done to me and her kids."

Forgiveness has been essential to Hope's healing process. She said, "My daughter is a changed person today. She is very active in NA and AA. We went out to lunch last week, and she made her amends to me. Did it make the past go away? No. What's done is done. But unless I chose to accept that and let the past go, there would always be a wedge between us. I didn't want that. Forgiveness is an act. Even if you don't feel it, you can say it. My main goal is not to get my addict well, but to get me well—not get her well and make myself sick in the process. Forgiveness is critical, not for the other person, but for yourself."

Hope added, "Forgiveness is an important part of any relationship. You have to stay on top of things so resentments don't build up. Days ago, I got angry at my daughter because she didn't do something I wanted her to do. I realized I was wrong and told her I was sorry."

Some families find it easier to forgive their addicted loved one than to forgive themselves. That has been my experience. Although I have certainly had flashes of anger toward my daughter, my overriding feelings toward her have been sorrow and love mingled with a good deal of self-recrimination. Looking back, I can see that I was not always a good parent, and although she has forgiven me, I have struggled to forgive myself. In this I am not alone. For example, Jack said that his healing process has included "admitting that I had a part to play in what happened to my son." According to him, "I felt a lot of self-blame. It's been tough to get past that."

Forgiving ourselves can be hard to do when we fear our actions have profoundly hurt someone we love. Jane said, "I felt a great deal of guilt and shame about the things I did that hurt my kids. I couldn't even say to them I was sorry because it was so much bigger than that. All I could do was just show up, be responsible, be there for them the way I should have been all along. I'm paying for college for my daughter. I'm doing everything I can to be a good mother to her and my son. Do I forgive myself? I'm working on it."

Some families continually beat themselves up because they fear they haven't done as much as they could have to save their loved one from addiction. They find it hard to forgive themselves for failing to do the impossible—getting another person clean and sober. Accepting responsibility for our mistakes and doing our best to make amends to those we have hurt is important. However, holding onto self-blame damages our sense of self-worth and limits our ability to heal.

Hope finds it helpful to put things in perspective when it comes to self-forgiveness. "I did the best I could for the time I was in," she said. "I am not perfect. I think a lot of us tend to be too hard on ourselves. I think we should be more gentle and stop beating ourselves up. If God can forgive us, we should be able to forgive ourselves." Hope's words echo a well-known truth: "To err is human, to forgive divine."

DEVELOPING YOUR SPIRITUAL CORE

Spirituality, as it applies to healing from the effects of addiction, does not necessarily include a Higher Power in our lives, although it can. It simply means taking steps to awaken the core of joy that is present in all human beings from the moment of birth. This may involve religion, nature, art, music, literature, helping others, or following any other life-affirming pursuit that connects us to something greater than ourselves.

When we are consumed with concern about our addicted loved one, our openness to the world shrivels. We tend to overlook what is beautiful in life and focus narrowly on what is frightening or tragic. Then we may conclude that the world is a terrible place or, at the very least, that our destiny is to suffer.

One woman said, "I only see the bad in things. If I think about my son's future, I see him winding up on the streets and eating out of Dumpsters. It never enters my mind to think that he might get better and live a wonderful life."

A husband said about his wife, "I worry constantly that she might start drinking again, even though she's been good for almost a year now. I can't appreciate her sobriety because I'm too afraid she's going to relapse."

Negative thoughts are inevitable in families of addicts. We've had a lot of negative experiences. It is easy for us to lose our faith and hope. If we are to heal, we must counteract the negative by nurturing our spirit. For Deb, this involved becoming active in a local theater group. "I love acting," she said. "Playing other characters helps me see how much there really is to life, how we all have our struggles. It helps put my own problems into perspective."

For Jack, developing his spirituality included taking long hikes in the mountains: "I'd always loved hiking, but I gave it up somehow or another. Now I try to get a good hike in at least once a week. There's something special about a view from a mountaintop. You get a sense that some things will last forever. I feel peace up there."

Hope's spiritual growth stemmed from strengthening her conscious contact with God. "God is a part of my everyday life now," she said. "I talk to him every day, and I trust him to take care of me and those I love. I have to listen and wait for his guidance. It can come in unexpected ways. For example, I remember sitting in a Nar-Anon meeting one night, feeling depressed as usual. A woman in the group was very funny, and she said something that made everyone laugh. I laughed too, and then I thought, 'Oh my God, I'm laughing. Maybe I'm not dead inside after all.' I hadn't laughed in years. Laughing felt strange, but it gave me a glimmer of light. I thought that maybe God wanted something more for me than to waste my life in self-pity. My advice to anyone who wants to heal is to trust any awakening you feel and keep building on it."

By trusting those glimmers of light and nurturing the things that give meaning and beauty to our lives, we help our spirits to heal and grow.

HEALING LESSONS

Someday far down the road, when the pain of facing addiction is not so raw and when we have begun our journey toward recovery and healing, we may come to regard the addiction of our loved one as a turning point that led us to embrace life on a deeper level. Every crisis presents an opportunity for personal growth, and facing the addiction of a loved one can help us to become stronger, more tolerant, and less judgmental.

As Jack expressed it, "I would never say I'm glad my son became addicted. But I'm thankful that as a result of his addiction, I've become a better person. There was a time when I might have looked at others who were having family problems and thought, 'Oh, what are you doing wrong? You must have done something to cause this.' Now I'm more compassionate. I know that terrible trouble can come to anyone."

Deb said, "I used to be very judgmental. I couldn't understand why people didn't just do things my way. Then everything would be all right. Now I believe that everyone is doing the best they can. You can't expect more than that."

Hope said, "Because addiction came into my life, I've become a little more accepting of other people, a little more understanding of what other people are feeling. It's also helped me put things in perspective. I don't have a lot of tolerance for the 'poor me' syndrome anymore. Instead of dwelling on what's not here, I keep a gratitude list. Sometimes it's an exercise to say, 'I trust you, God.' But I have faith. I have some peace. This is life."

What Jack, Deb, Hope, and many others have learned is that addiction is a devastating experience both for addicted individuals and for those who love them. Few things in life are more painful than watching substance abuse steal our loved ones away from us. But addiction is also an experience from which addicts and their families can emerge stronger and wiser than they were before. Many recovering addicts, including my own daughter, become people of great compassion, humility, and generosity. Many recovering families of addicts develop similar strengths of character.

Addiction, like cancer, is not a disease that can be cured. There is never a point in time when we can say it is all over;

the battle has been won. But it is a disease from which important lessons can be learned. If from among those lessons we learn how to live our own lives to the best of our ability and acquire the grace to allow others to do the same, then something immeasurably precious will have been won.

APPENDIX A

SYMPTOMS AND EFFECTS OF MAJOR
ADDICTIVE SUBSTANCES

All psychoactive substances achieve their effects by changing the body's natural chemical balance. Although the chemistry and neurobiology involved is extremely complex and not yet fully understood by scientists, the following chemicals seem to be major players in the addiction process.

Dopamine: A neurotransmitter that is plentiful in the brain's reward circuit. It is the brain's primary pleasure messenger.

Endorphins: Chains of protein-building blocks. These morphinelike neurotransmitters reduce pain, alleviate stress, and promote pleasure.

Gamma-aminobutyric acid (GABA): This neurotransmitter quiets the brain by blocking stimulation, including anxiety and worry.

Norepinephrine: Similar to adrenaline, this neurotransmitter affects heart rate and blood pressure and is involved in the body's natural fight or flight response to emergencies.

Serotonin: Only 2 percent of the body's serotonin is found in the brain as a neurotransmitter, but this chemical affects motor function, pain perception, appetite, and the sympathetic nervous system, which is not subject to voluntary control.

The pleasurable effects of nonmedical psychoactive substances are profound but generally short term. And because the brain always strives to achieve a balance, when the initial effects begin to wear off, the exact opposite effects begin to occur. Withdrawal from a depressant will generally produce agitation, and withdrawal from a stimulant will lead to exhaustion. Addicts must use with regularity to sustain the pleasurable effects of the drug and avoid the negative effects of withdrawal.

Following is an overview of the major psychoactive addictive substances widely available today. This listing contains a simplified account of the chemical properties of each substance, its effects on the user, symptoms of use and withdrawal, and paraphernalia associated with its use.

Alcohol is produced by a chemical reaction between fermenting enzymes (most often from yeast) and sugars or starches from plant products. The enzymes split complex organic matter into simple substances, in this case, sugar into carbon dioxide and alcohol. Fermentation stops naturally when the alcohol concentration in the mixture reaches about 12 percent.

A much higher concentration of alcohol is achieved through the process of distillation. Heating fermented products to create vapors and then cooling and collecting the vapors makes whiskey, gin, rum, and other hard liquors. The amount of alcohol is measured by "proof" in the United States. The proof number is twice the percent of alcohol in a given liquor. Thus, ninety-proof whiskey is 45 percent alcohol.

The type of alcohol contained in beer, wine, and hard liquors is identical: pure ethyl alcohol. Although some beer or wine drinkers believe that their drinks are less intoxicating than mixed drinks, they are mistaken. A twelve-ounce glass of beer, about five ounces of wine, and about one-and-a-half ounces of distilled liquor contain equivalent amounts of alcohol: about one-half ounce. Furthermore, the short-term and long-term effects of these drinks are the same.

Although alcohol immediately acts as a stimulant, it is in fact a depressant drug. The initial alcohol high is caused by a surge of dopamine, serotonin, epinephrine (related to norepinephrine), and endorphins. Alcohol also stimulates the release of GABA. The result of this chemical cocktail is a sensation of warmth and well-being and a lessening of inhibitions, which explains why people under the influence will often do or say things they later find embarrassing. Drinkers may display unusual affection or express grandiose ideas as the early stages of intoxication take hold. Eventually, the quieting effects of GABA will cause drinkers to feel relaxed and sleepy. But heavy alcohol consumption disrupts normal brain function, leading to anxiety, sleeplessness, and nightmares as withdrawal sets in.

Alcohol in low doses is generally harmless, although the artificially induced sense of well-being may impair judgment and slow reflex time, leading to serious accidents. Additionally, habitual drinking of even small doses can eventually lead to the release of anger and irritability. It is not uncommon for routine evening drinkers to unleash their dissatisfaction with the world as the alcohol strips away their inhibitions. In larger doses, alcohol affects motor skills, causing loss of coordination and slurred speech; irritates the stomach lining; and triggers the body's vomiting mechanism.

Another consequence of heavy drinking is a blackout, an episode in which the drinker looks and acts relatively normal but is highly intoxicated. The drinker will later have no memory of what was done or said during that period. A single episode of heavy drinking can also produce loss of consciousness, a coma, or even death.

There is no precise measure of the difference between harmless social drinking, excessive drinking, and alcoholism (full-blown addiction). One guideline suggests that the "safe" number of drinks per week is seven for women and eleven for men. In his book *The Selfish Brain,* Dr. Robert DuPont says that routinely having more than four drinks a week may be cause for concern (p. 289). Regardless of the quantity of alcohol consumed, when alcohol produces changed moods and behaviors or blackouts, and when it begins to interfere with daily life, a line has been crossed. Then the drinking has become problematic and should be treated.

Not all problem drinkers exhibit the more obvious signs of alcohol abuse. I have known people who regularly consume a six-pack or more of sixteen-ounce beers every night and yet show no outward signs of intoxication. This is not remarkable among heavy drinkers. Most alcoholics can "hold their liquor"; that is, they exhibit only minor effects from heavy drinking. They have conditioned their brains to function reasonably well with alcohol present. This learned condition causes many heavy drinkers to believe that alcohol does not affect them. But prolonged heavy use of alcohol takes its toll whether or not the effects are immediately apparent.

The physical consequences of long-term alcohol abuse begin with the liver, where alcohol is broken down into carbon dioxide and water. The liver can be damaged in three progressively serious ways: (1) normal red liver tissue is replaced with yellow fat; (2) liver hepatitis develops, which means that the inflamed liver malfunctions, leading to yellowing of the eyes and skin (jaundice); (3) cirrhosis of the liver occurs, in which normal tissue is replaced by white scar tissue. The cirrhotic liver cannot do its job of cleaning the blood, leading to blood poisoning and other life-threatening conditions. Cirrhosis of the liver is nonreversible, although the progress of the disease may stop if drinking ceases. In its advanced stages, cirrhosis is fatal.

In addition to liver disease, long-term heavy drinking produces other physical impairments. Alcohol often irritates the gastro-intestinal tract and can inflame the esophagus and stomach, aggravating peptic ulcer disease. It can inflame the pancreas, leading to chronic acute pancreatitis. This condition produces a knifelike pain in the middle abdomen and can be fatal. Alcoholism can result in permanent brain degeneration, including paralysis of nerves and memory loss. It can also lead to anemia, cardiovascular diseases, and degeneration of the heart muscle. As if all this were not enough, alcohol abuse also contributes to cancer of the mouth, esophagus, stomach, larynx, liver, and lung. Babies born to alcoholic mothers often suffer from fetal alcohol syndrome (FAS), a combination of permanent physical and mental defects.

Habitual heavy drinkers may even experience severe withdrawal if the drinking stops abruptly. This potentially fatal condition, known as delirium tremens (D.T.'s), may induce high fever, hallucinations, and seizures.

Alcoholism is a progressive disease that causes severe physical and mental damage over time. Early indicators of alcohol abuse, in addition to the well-recognized effects of intoxication, include alcohol odor on the breath or excreted by sweat glands, bleary eyes, chronic stomachaches or pain, facial yellowing and/or puffiness, shakiness and irritability in the mornings, loss of appetite, frequent accidents, blackouts, and sudden and inexplicable mood swings.

Evidence of use: a steady stock of alcohol in the house, empty cans or bottles, hidden cans or bottles—full or empty

Marijuana consists of the flowering tops, leaves, and stems of the plant *Cannabis sativa.* Unlike alcohol, cocaine, and heroin, which are refined, or processed, agricultural products consisting of a single chemical, marijuana is used in its crude, natural state. The dried plant contains more than 420 different chemicals, while marijuana smoke contains more than 2,000. The chemical most responsible for the marijuana high is delta-9-tetrahydrocannabinol (THC). THC receptors are widely distributed throughout the brain, with higher concentrations in the cerebellum and hippocampus, regions involved with motor function, learning, and memory. The brain's pleasure centers are connected to these areas, but scientists have yet to determine the natural function of the

neurotransmitter that matches THC. It is known that THC stimulates the norepinephrine transmitter system, and there are indica-
tions that it may also affect levels of GABA and serotonin.

Although the precise mechanics of the marijuana high are still
unclear, the effects of using marijuana are well documented. The
drug sedates the brain and alters mental processes. The ability to
learn, concentrate, and remember is diminished; reaction time is
slowed; and perception of time and distance is distorted. Appetite
and thirst may increase, and in larger doses, marijuana may induce
irritability, paranoia, anxiety, and panic.

Long-term marijuana use has been linked to permanent brain
cell and chromosomal damage, impaired reasoning skills, respiratory illnesses, reduced fertility, miscarriages, and, when used during pregnancy, fetal alcohol syndrome (FAS). Perhaps the most
widely recognized effect of heavy marijuana use is a condition
commonly known as burnout. The user exhibits obvious mental
impairments combined with a lack of motivation, purpose, or
will. Drug counselors often use the term *amotivational syndrome* to
describe this condition, which is typical of many habitual marijuana users.

Marijuana is usually smoked. The chemicals are inhaled into the
lungs and then carried in the bloodstream to all the body's cells.
Because THC is fat soluble and not water soluble, it is not easily
eliminated from the body but is instead retained in the brain, re-
productive glands, and other fat-containing tissues of the body for
days or even weeks. Studies have shown that the retained THC can
impair memory for six weeks or longer after marijuana is used.

There is some debate about whether marijuana is technically
an addictive drug, since it generally produces no physical withdrawal symptoms. There is no question, however, that heavy marijuana use leads to physical and psychological dependence and that
compulsive use of the drug can persist despite severe negative
consequences.

Evidence of use: small seeds, stems, and leaves resembling dried basil; pipes, bongs (water pipes), and rolling paper (sold for rolling cigarettes but usually used for rolling joints); small flattened remains of marijuana cigarettes (roaches); ash that does not smell like tobacco; burn holes in clothing, bedding, furniture, or car seats; the distinctive smell of marijuana smoke; dilated pupils and bloodshot eyes

Cocaine is made from coca leaves grown in the Andes Mountains of South America. To isolate the active ingredient, producers soak and mash the leaves into a paste, which is 60 to 80 percent pure cocaine. It is generally distributed in salt form, known as cocaine hydrochloride. This fine, white powder, which resembles snow, is usually snorted up the nose through a straw, rolled dollar bill, or devices made specifically for this purpose (known as bullets). It can also be injected.

In the 1980s, a more potent form of the drug was developed: crack cocaine. Heating cocaine hydrochloride in a solution of baking soda until the water evaporates produces crack. The resultant rocks or pellets are heated with a flame to produce vapors that are inhaled. High levels of crack hit the brain within eight seconds of being smoked, delivering the fastest and most powerful high of any drug. (Drugs used intravenously reach the brain in about sixteen seconds.)

Because a cocaine high is so fleeting, lasting less than an hour, the drug is usually taken in "runs." Users take repeated hits every few minutes for hours or even days. They pursue their initial euphoria with manic compulsion. However, with each repeated use, the high becomes less and less satisfying because of chemical reactions within the brain.

Cocaine, like all stimulant drugs, affects the body's central nervous system, increasing heart rate and blood pressure. It triggers the release of norepinephrine and promotes sensations of alertness, confidence, and energy. But cocaine's real kick comes from its effects on the dopamine system.

In a cocaine-free brain, most dopamine neurotransmitters return to be used again and again. A few of them, however, are broken down by naturally occurring enzymes. The body gradually creates new dopamine to maintain a balance within the brain. This natural process is disrupted by cocaine, which traps dopamine in the synapses for an abnormally long time, causing euphoria and an exaggerated sensation of well-being. As the brain gets locked in this supercharged state, sleep becomes impossible and hunger is suppressed.

The natural enzymes then break down dopamine in large quantities, faster than it can be produced. Dopamine loss sets in. By the time the cocaine run stops, little dopamine is left in the brain. The user feels tired and often intensely depressed. The brain can take months to reestablish a normal dopamine balance, and prolonged heavy cocaine abuse may permanently damage the dopamine system, diminishing the addict's capacity to experience any pleasure at all.

Among substances of abuse, cocaine is distinctive because of its diminishing returns. Most addicts of other substances start using to achieve the euphoric feelings associated with initial use; however, they continue using in order to feel "normal." Heavy cocaine use never creates a feeling of normalcy. Instead it causes panic, paranoia, aggression, and not uncommonly, psychotic episodes. It distorts judgment and twists perceptions, effects that can last for weeks or even months after it was last used. Some users experience "coke bugs," a disturbing sensation that bugs are burrowing under their skin. They may try to dig them out with their fingernails, creating open sores on their bodies. Babies born to crack-addicted mothers often suffer severe developmental handicaps.

Cocaine produces no clearly defined withdrawal symptoms, and users are not compelled to use their drug daily, unlike alcoholics and heroin addicts. But it is highly addictive. The compulsion to use becomes irresistible, and the search for the cocaine high becomes so compelling that most addicts can't stop until their world crashes down around them.

Evidence of use: plastic baggies; fine, white powder that numbs the tongue if tasted; bullets, or specially made devices that are used to measure out a dose of cocaine and fit into the nostrils; pea-size brownish pellets (crack); crack pipes, often made by sticking a straw in a plastic bottle and placing tinfoil on the open end; blackened fingernails and decayed front teeth (indicates crack use); constantly running nose (indicates cocaine use); wads of tissues or paper towels in pockets (for runny nose); nonstop talking; physical agitation; extreme lethargy

Heroin is morphine (a narcotic derived from opium poppies) combined with two activating chemicals (acetyl groups) that speed up the drug's entry into the brain's synapses. Once in the brain, the acetyl groups fall off, leaving the morphine molecules to work their effects. (Morphine, not heroin, is found in urine tests of heroin users.) Street heroin is combined with nonactive substances such as starch, powdered milk, sugar, or quinine. It is a soft, fine powder resembling talc and ranging in color from off-white to dark brown. It is commonly sold in approximately one-by-two-inch bags of opaque paper. The bags are sealed on both ends and up the back and stamped on the front with a colored pattern: the dealer's stamp.

Heroin is usually injected intravenously, although purer, more potent forms of the drug now make it possible to get high by snorting it. Snorting is how many people today are introduced to heroin, because snorting does not carry the same stigma as intravenous drug use. As addiction takes hold, however, most users graduate to the more powerful method of injecting.

To prepare for intravenous use, the user dissolves the heroin by adding it to water in a spoon or bottle cap, then heating it with a match or lighter. To prevent undissolved particles from entering the bloodstream, users may place cotton or a piece of cigarette filter in the liquid before drawing it up into the needle.

Whether snorted or injected, heroin stimulates the release of dopamine and acts directly acts on the brain's natural opiate receptors (the endorphin system). The result is a sensation of warmth, a powerful rush of pleasure followed by a sense of calm and contentment. (Inexperienced users may vomit with initial heroin use, but this reaction disappears as tolerance develops.) Heroin, like all opiate-based substances, eases pain and distress by inhibiting the transmission of pain-carrying impulses. As a depressant, it affects most major systems of the body. It slows the respiratory system, lowers blood pressure, suppresses coughs, slows bowel function (leading to constipation), reduces appetite and sex drive, minimizes aggression, and interferes with normal menstrual cycles.

The immediate effect of heroin is a warm glow. The user's face may be flushed and shiny, the nose and eyes may be runny, and the pupils may be constricted. Severe itching may also occur. A pleasant, languid drowsiness takes hold, causing the user to "nod," a condition resembling sleep in which the upper eyelids droop and the mouth hangs open. This phase is followed by a period of calm during which there are few observable changes in the user's appearance or behavior. Unlike abusers of alcohol, marijuana, and cocaine, heroin addicts can use for a long time before being detected if they have access to a steady supply of their drug.

The effects of heroin last for several hours before withdrawal begins. Because it is physically addicting and affects every part of the body, even the bones, heroin withdrawal is extremely uncomfortable. Addicts experience nausea, severe aches and pains, sweating, insomnia, panic, depression, cramping, and diarrhea. Their behavior becomes anxious and agitated as they begin their search for the next fix.

Heroin withdrawal, unlike alcohol or barbiturate withdrawal, is rarely life threatening. Nevertheless, heroin addiction may have serious consequences, including death from overdose. Overdose deaths most often happen with addicts who use after a period of abstinence, which lowers their tolerance level. Doses that they could previously tolerate may now prove lethal. Unusually pure forms of the drug may also cause overdose, as may a simple mistake in calculating how much of the drug is being taken. Other health risks include HIV infection from sharing needles, collapsed veins from repeated injections, serious infections at injection sites, and hepatitis, an incurable and potentially fatal disease that damages the liver. Pregnant users risk miscarriages and stillbirths, and infants who do survive are born addicted and experience painful withdrawal symptoms.

Evidence of use: off-white or brownish bitter-tasting powder; scabs and scarring on veins, especially on the arms and hands; "kits" or "works" consisting of a syringe, a spoon or bottle cap, a tourniquet (to enlarge veins for injection), matches or a lighter, and cotton balls or cigarette filters that are shredded or cut into disks; tissues with blood spots; spots of blood on inner sleeves or cuffs; cigarette holes on clothes, bedding, car seats, or furniture (from smoking while nodding); flushed face; constricted pupils; watery eyes and nose; itching; extreme lethargy or agitation

In addition to the four major substance of abuse, there are many other natural and synthetic substances that alter brain chemistry. Here is a brief overview of the most commonly abused.

Amphetamines and methamphetamines are synthetic stimulants (also known as speed) that mimic cocaine but with much longer-lasting effects. Taken orally, smoked, or injected, stimulants produce a burst of energy that can quickly turn to paranoia and violence.

Hallucinogens may be synthetic or natural compounds and include lysergic acid diethylamide (LSD), psilocybin mushrooms, Ecstasy, and phencyclidine (PCP). Taken orally, hallucinogens inhibit the release of serotonin and alter mood, thought, and perception. Sensory input becomes jumbled and distorted; the brain loses its ability to perceive reality; and anxiety, panic, and psychosis may result.

Nicotine, the addictive substance in tobacco, stimulates the release of dopamine and norepinephrine. Although it does not produce intoxication or mental impairment, it does elevate heart rate and blood pressure and poses severe health threats. According to *The Women's Complete Wellness Book,* cigarettes are responsible for approximately one out of every five deaths in the United States today—more than the total deaths from alcohol and illicit drugs combined.

Prescription drugs may contain chemicals that act as stimulants or depressants and thus may be abused. Stimulants include Ritalin, Cylert, Preludin, Tenuate, and lonamin. Depressants include Nembutal, Seconal, Amytal, and tuinals. Opiate-based depressants include codeine, pethidine, Demerol, paregoric, Percocet, Percodan, Tussionex, Darvon, Talwin, Lomotil, OxyContin, and fentanyl.

APPENDIX B

WORDS OF WISDOM

Loving an addict is almost certain to produce many anxious moments. Here are some meditations and slogans heard in Twelve Step programs, as well as words of wisdom from others who have been there.

The Serenity Prayer
God, grant me the serenity
to accept the things I cannot change,
courage to change the things I can,
and wisdom to know the difference.

- Faith is the substance of things hoped for, the evidence of things not seen. (Heb. 2:1)
- You didn't cause it, you can't control it, and you can't cure it.
- If nothing changes, nothing changes.
- Progress, not perfection.
- God's never in a hurry, but he's always on time.
- In God's time, not my time.
- One day at a time.
- In nature there are no rewards or punishments. There are consequences.

- First things first.
- Live and let live.
- Easy does it.
- How important is it?
- Keep it simple.
- There but for the grace of God go I.
- Let go and let God.
- One day at a time.
- This, too, shall pass.
- Recovery is a journey, not a destination.
- Keep an open mind.
- Decisions aren't forever.
- It takes time.
- Change is a process, not an event.
- Fear is the darkroom where negatives are developed.
- Before engaging your mouth, put your mind in gear.
- There is no chemical solution to a spiritual problem.
- Spirituality is the ability to get our minds off ourselves.
- The first step in overcoming mistakes is to admit them.
- Formula for failure: trying to please everyone.
- A journey of a thousand miles begins with a single step.
- Trying to pray is praying.
- We're responsible for the effort, not the outcome.
- Minds are like parachutes—they won't work unless they're open.
- It isn't the load that weighs us down; it's the way we carry it.
- Serenity is not freedom from the storm but peace amid the storm.
- The seven Ts: take time to think the thing through.
- The results are in God's hands.
- We are not human beings having spiritual experiences; we are spiritual beings having human experiences.

- It's a pity we can't forget our troubles the same way we forget our blessings.
- Active addicts don't have relationships; they take hostages.
- Every day is a gift; that is why we call it the present.
- Recovery works for people who believe in God; recovery works for people who don't believe in God. Recovery never works for people who believe they *are* God.
- Just for today I will try to live through this day only and not tackle my whole life problems at once. I can do something for twelve hours that would appall me if I felt that I had to keep it up for a lifetime.
- There are two days in every week over which we have no control: yesterday and tomorrow. Today is the only day we can change.
- Pain is the touchstone of spiritual growth.
- The road to disappointment is paved with expectations.
- Depression is anger turned inward.

APPENDIX C

RESOURCES

Local chapters of Alcoholics Anonymous, Narcotics Anonymous, Al-Anon, and Nar-Anon can be found in most communities. They are all good sources of information and support. Additionally, private and public agencies that treat substance abuse usually offer educational materials and programs for families. For more information, contact any of the following organizations:

Al-Anon Family Group Headquarters, Inc.
1600 Corporate Landing Parkway
Virginia Beach, VA 23454-5617
(757) 563-1600; (888) 4AL-ANON (meeting information)
www.al-anon.alateen.org

Alcoholics Anonymous World Services, Inc.
General Service Office
P.O. Box 459
Grand Central Station
New York, NY 10163
(212) 870-3400
www.aa.org

Betty Ford Center
39000 Bob Hope Drive
Rancho Mirage, CA 92270
(760) 773-4100; (800) 854-9211
www.bettyfordcenter.org

Center for Substance Abuse Treatment (CSAT)
Substance Abuse and Mental Health Services Administration
    (SAMHSA)
5600 Fishers Lane
Rockville, MD 20857
(301) 443-8956; (800) 662-HELP (treatment and support
    group referral)
www.samhsa.gov/centers/csat2002/csat_frame.html

Families Anonymous, Inc.
P.O. Box 3475
Culver City, CA 90231-3475
(800) 736-9805
www.familiesanonymous.org

Federation of Families for Children's Mental Health
1101 King Street, Suite 420
Alexandria, VA 22314
(703) 684-7710
www.ffcmh.org

Hazelden
15245 Pleasant Valley Road
P.O. Box 11
Center City, MN 55012-0011
(800) 257-7810
www.hazelden.org

Nar-Anon Family Group Headquarters, Inc.
302 West Fifth Street, Suite 301
San Pedro, CA 90731
(310) 547-5800
www.onlinerecovery.org/co/nfg/

Narcotics Anonymous World Services, Inc.
P.O. Box 9999
Van Nuys, CA 91409
(818) 773-9999
www.na.org

National Clearinghouse for Alcohol and Drug Information (NCADI)
P.O. Box 2345
Rockville, MD 20852-2345
(800) 729-6686; (301) 468-2600
www.health.org

National Council on Alcoholism and Drug Dependence, Inc.
  (NCADD)
20 Exchange Place, Suite 2902
New York, NY 10005
(212) 269-7797; (800) NCA-CALL (twenty-four-hour
  referral line)
www.ncadd.org

National Families in Action (NFIA)
2957 Clairmont Road Northeast, Suite 150
Atlanta, GA 30329
(404) 248-9676
www.nationalfamilies.org

APPENDIX D

RECOMMENDED READING

For further reading on addiction and recovery, the following materials may be helpful:

Blamed and Ashamed: The Treatment Experiences of Youth with Co-occurring Substance Abuse and Mental Health Disorders and Their Families. Alexandria, Va.: Federation of Families for Children's Mental Health and Keys for Networking, 2001.

Colleran, Carol, and Debra Jay. *Aging and Addiction: Helping Older Adults Overcome Alcohol or Medication Dependence.* Center City, Minn.: Hazelden, 2002.

DuPont, Robert L. *The Selfish Brain: Learning from Addiction.* Center City, Minn.: Hazelden, 1997.

Hardiman, Michael. *Overcoming Addiction: A Common Sense Approach.* Freedom, Calif.: Crossing Press, 2000.

Jay, Jeff, and Debra Jay. *Love First: A New Approach to Intervention for Alcoholism and Drug Addiction.* Center City, Minn.: Hazelden, 2000.

McGovern, George. *Terry: My Daughter's Life-and-Death Struggle with Alcoholism.* New York: Villard Books, 1996.

Nakken, Craig. *Reclaim Your Family from Addiction: How Couples and Families Recover Love and Meaning.* Center City, Minn.: Hazelden, 2000.

Pepper, Bert, M.D., Hilary Ryglewicz, and Jackie Massaro. *Alcohol, Street Drugs, and Emotional Problems: What You Need to Know.* Center City, Minn.: Hazelden, 2003.

Prochaska, James O., John C. Norcross, and Carlo C. DiClemente. *Changing for Good.* New York: William Morrow, 1994.

Ryglewicz, Hilary, and Bert Pepper. *Lives at Risk: Understanding and Treating Young People with Dual Disorders.* New York: Free Press, 1996.

Ryglewicz, Hilary, Bert Pepper, and Jackie Massaro. *Alcohol, Street Drugs, and Emotional Problems: What the Family Needs to Know.* Center City, Minn.: Hazelden, 2003.

ABOUT THE AUTHOR

Beverly Conyers has worked as a teacher and freelance writer for the past ten years. An avid gardener, she lives with her dog and two cats in the Northeast. She continues to be active in Twelve Step recovery programs.